MONKEY
TRAPS

WHY EVERYBODY TRIES TO CONTROL
EVERYTHING AND HOW WE CAN STOP

Steve Hau
illustrated by t

MONKEYTRAPS
Why Everybody Tries to Control
Everything and How We Can Stop

ISBN 978-1-61961-380-5

LIONCREST
PUBLISHING

For Chris:
Best editor, best friend,
and coauthor in all
the good stuff.

CONTENTS

INTRODUCTION

Want to trap a monkey?

Try this:

1. Find a heavy bottle with a narrow neck.

2. Drop a banana into it.

3. Leave the bottle where a monkey can find it.

4. Wait.

The monkey will do the rest.

He'll come along, smell the banana, reach in to grab it.

Then find he can't pull it out because the bottleneck is too small.

He can free himself easily. He just has to let go.

But he really really wants that banana.

So he hangs on.

He's still hanging on when you come to collect him.

And that's how you trap a monkey.

*   *   *

Want to trap a human being?

Try this:

1. Place the human being in an uncomfortable situation.

2. Wait.

The human will do the rest.

Humans will try to reduce their discomfort by controlling the situation.

The harder they work to reduce their discomfort, the more uncomfortable they'll get.

The harder they try to escape their discomfort, the more trapped they'll feel.

And that's how you trap a human being.

*   *   *

This is a book about control in general, and psychological monkeytraps in particular.

A *psychological monkeytrap* is any situation that tempts us to hold on when we should let go—to control what either cannot or should not be controlled.

The world is filled with monkeytraps.

As is the emotional life of every human being.

I learned this from practicing psychotherapy.

Practicing therapy also taught me four truths:

1. *We are all addicted to control.*

2. *This addiction causes most (maybe all) of our emotional problems.*

3. *Behind this addiction lies our wish to control feelings.*

4. *There are better ways to manage feelings than control.*

I call these the Four Laws of Control and they organize the four parts that follow:

Part 1: Addiction is about the idea of control and how it structures our lives and choices.

Part 2: Dysfunction is about the most common ways control addiction makes us (and those we love) sick and miserable.

Part 3: Emotion is about the real reason we try to control people, places, things, and ourselves.

Part 4: Plan B is about moving beyond control addiction to healthier ways of handling our feelings and living our lives.

*   *   *

Finally:

You may be used to thinking of control as a solution, not a problem.

Fine. Read on.

You may not think of yourself as a *controlling* person.

Also fine. Read on.

You may never have tried redefining your emotional problems as rooted in your wish for control.

Terrific. Read on.

A client once described his first Al-Anon meeting as "like a light coming on in a dark room. Suddenly I could see all the furniture I've been tripping over all my life."

That's just what we're going for here.

Welcome to the light switch.

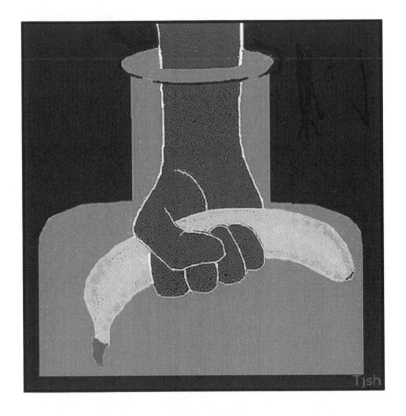

PART I

ADDICTION

The idea of control controls the controllers; we
are not in control of the power of control.

— JAMES HILLMAN

CONTROL

The ability to dictate reality.

That's how I define control.

It's not a definition you'll find in any dictionary, and probably not how you define it.

But it's essential to understanding everything that follows.

Dictate means rearrange or edit according to our preferences. *Reality* means, well, everything—everything outside us (people, places, and things) and inside us (thoughts, feelings, behavior) as well.

Defined this broadly, the wish for control stands behind just about everything we do consciously, plus most of what we do unconsciously (feel, fantasize, dream, worry about) as well.

We seek control in order to get reality to behave as we want it to.

We seek control because we want to make the world adjust itself to us, instead of vice versa.

We all want control in this sense.

Not just want, either.

We *crave* it.

Control is the mother of all motivations.

Every human ever born has craved it and chased it.

Because it's a craving that is literally built into us.

CONTROLLING

The urge to control is part of our hard wiring.

Why?

Because it is wired into us to:

- Seek pleasure and avoid pain,

- Imagine a perfect life (one that meets all our needs and makes us perfectly happy), and then

- Try to make what we imagine come true.

The word *controlling* covers all forms of this imagining and trying.

Our trying may be large (building a skyscraper) or small (killing crabgrass), complex (winning a war) or simple (salting our soup).

It may be important (curing cancer) or petty (trimming toenails); public (getting elected) or private (losing weight); essential (avoiding a car crash) or incidental (matching socks).

I may inflict my trying on other people (get you to kiss me, stop drinking, wash the dishes, give me a raise) or on myself (lose weight, raise my self-esteem, hide my anger, learn French).

All this involves seeking some form of control.

We're controlling nearly all of the time.

We control automatically and unconsciously, waking and sleeping, out in the world and in the privacy of our thoughts.

From birth until death.

The only time we're *not* controlling is when we can relax, and do nothing, and trust that things will work out just fine anyway.

And how often can you do that?

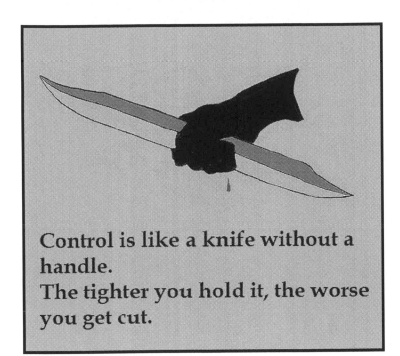

Control is like a knife without a handle.
The tighter you hold it, the worse you get cut.

PICTURES

You may not think of yourself as controlling.

Well, you are.

You just don't see it.

Consider this view of how we operate:

From moment to moment, each of us carries in our heads a picture of the reality we want. And we're constantly comparing that internal picture to the reality we have.

Everything we do to bring those pictures closer together— whether we do it out in public or in the privacy of our most secret thoughts—is what I mean by *controlling*.

See it yet?

Add this, then:

Discomfort of any sort—physical, mental, emotional, spiritual, everything from agony to an itch—amounts to a signal that the two pictures don't match.

And we respond to that signal automatically.

So wherever there's discomfort, there's controlling.

And we all know how uncomfortable life can be.

Controlling, in short, is as reflexive and inevitable a response as slapping a mosquito that's biting you.

See it now?

CHAMELEON

Controlling is hard to spot and even harder to talk about.

Several reasons for this:

1. *It's automatic and unconscious,* like blinking or the beat of a heart. You can make yourself aware of your own controlling, but it takes effort.

2. *It's normal.* You do it all the time. Everyone around you does it all the time. So controlling behavior fades into the background of awareness, like a chameleon blends into its surroundings.

3. *We use stunted language to describe it.* We apply the verb *control* to wildly different behaviors, to our handling of

everything from feelings to finances, foreign trade to cholesterol, termites to acne. We almost need to construct a new language in order to adequately describe this elusive chameleon.

Let's try to do that, then.

Control addiction is like a teddy bear with razor blades in its fur.

We hug it for comfort, and only later notice that we're bleeding.

A CONTROLLING PERSON

Start with an experiment.

In the privacy of your own mind, take a moment to consider this question:

> *How does a controlling person look, sound, and act?*

(Authorial pause while reader complies.)

What came up?

If you bothered to try this I'm guessing you found some image, memory, or feeling that carries the emotional weight of the word *controlling* for you.

What most of us encounter is a distillation of our most powerful (usually most painful) experiences with people by whom we've felt controlled.

Or we discover that we harbor some archetypal image of how *a controlling person* looks and acts, someone like Hitler, or Donald Trump, or Mom.

That, at least, used to be my own reaction.

It changed when I began to really study control.

Ten years of practicing a therapy focused mainly on control issues taught me to see controlling as a shape-shifter, so various, subtle and relentless that it manages to slip sideways into virtually every experience and interaction.

And I came to see the need for some finer distinctions.

Some first steps, then, towards a more descriptive language.

EXTERNAL AND INTERNAL

Let's start by distinguishing different types of controlling.

To begin with, controlling may be external or internal.

External controlling focuses outside the individual, on people, places, and things. *Internal* controlling focuses inside the individual, on his or her own thoughts, feelings, and behavior.

Cleaning my garage, disciplining my kids, selling anyone anything, and steering my car out of a skid are examples of external controlling.

Dieting, memorizing French verbs, learning to meditate, and hiding my true feelings are examples of internal controlling.

This may seem an obvious distinction. It isn't.

That's because people addicted to control often lose the ability to distinguish between external and internal.

For example, let's say that I—like most control addicts—believe that the only way to achieve self-acceptance (internal) is to get you to like me or love me or admire me (external). So I try to control you in order to control how I feel.

But I may also be convinced that in order to control you (external), I must control myself (internal)—lose weight, be funny, drive a nice car, or hide what I really think of your haircut or your politics.

So I control *you* in order to control *me*, and I control *me* in order to control *you*.

And if you're a control addict, you do the same.

And the boundary between us gets impossibly blurred.

(More on this confusion later, in **Part 2: Dysfunction**.)

OVERT AND COVERT

Controlling may also be overt or covert.

Overt controlling is observable or obvious. *Covert* controlling is hidden or disguised.

When I direct my son to take out the garbage, that's overt controlling. When he forgets and I retaliate by scowling or refusing to talk to him, that's covert.

Remember *All in the Family*? Archie Bunker's treatment of his wife ("Stifle yourself, you dingbat") was overtly controlling. But Edith controlled Archie right back—by shutting her mouth, agreeing with him, bringing him a beer. She used people-pleasing to manage Archie and manipulate him out of his bad moods. And manipulation is another name for covert controlling.

Most of our controlling is covert.

Do you ever lie? Go along to get along?

Hide your true thoughts and feelings? Tell people what you think they want to hear?

Laugh at jokes you find unfunny? Act politely towards people you hate?

Take better care of others than of yourself?

All covert controlling.

Covert controlling is, in fact, the universal social lubricant.

It's how socialized human beings relate to each other.

Universal. Inevitable. Inescapable.

Like a psychological sea in which everyone swims.

CONSCIOUS AND UNCONSCIOUS

Controlling can be conscious or unconscious.

Conscious controlling is the sort we notice ourselves doing. *Unconscious* controlling operates outside our awareness.

Archie probably knew he was trying to control Edith. Edith, though, may not have realized she was controlling him back.

One way we hide our controlling from ourselves is by calling it something else: *politeness, helpfulness, consideration, respect, being nice.* But those words often disguise our real motivation.

That's not to say all unconscious controlling is dishonest or unhealthy. But it's also true that the vast majority of compulsive controllers are relentlessly "nice" people unaware of their driving need for control.

They're also unaware of how much their need for control controls them.

It's easy to identify such people. Just place them in a situation beyond their control and see how uncomfortable they get.

On the wall behind my chair there's a picture of flowers. I once tilted it so that it hung crooked. Then I spent the day watching my clients' eyes flick back and forth between my face and the crooked picture. Most were unaware they were doing this. All seemed increasingly uneasy or restless as our sessions progressed. Two finally felt compelled to ask permission to straighten my picture.

Control addicts are people who don't know what they're doing and insist on their right to keep doing it.

FUNCTIONAL AND DYSFUNCTIONAL

Perhaps most importantly:

Controlling may be functional or dysfunctional.

Functional controlling is healthy controlling, in some way necessary, appropriate, or need-satisfying.

Dysfunctional controlling—also called *dyscontrol*—is none of those things.

Distinguishing the two can be tricky. Dyscontrol often seems, in the moment, to be an effective way of coping.

Remember the list of controlling behaviors I offered in chapter 7? (*Do you ever lie? Go along to get along?*) Most of us find it impossible to never engage in some of that stuff.

But eventually all forms of dyscontrol fail.

That's because where functional controlling represents an attempt to face and solve a problem, dyscontrol is a fear-based response whose main goal is to avoid anxiety or discomfort.

We'll examine specific examples of this in **Part 2: Dysfunction**.

For now it's enough to define *dyscontrol* as any controlling that ends up frustrating needs instead of meeting them.

Even Edith Bunker came to recognize this. Eventually she saw she needed to stand up to Archie, to stop appeasing him and simply say No.

(Haven't watched that particular episode? Please do. Search YouTube for *All in the Family*, Season 6, Episode 89, "Edith Breaks Out" and jump to 12:30. And notice the studio audience's reaction.)

CHOICEFUL AND COMPULSIVE

There's one more important distinction to make.

It is closely related to the last one, but essential to understand in its own right:

Controlling may be choiceful or compulsive.

By *choiceful* I mean both conscious and freely chosen. *Compulsive* means driven by anxiety, to where a person essentially loses the ability to choose.

Most dysfunctional controlling is compulsive.

Compulsive controllers are people who see no other way to feel safe or secure than by trying to control people, places, things, and themselves, and who keep on controlling despite all evidence that the control they seek is an illusion.

Another word for compulsive is *addictive*.

Compulsive controllers, then, are addicts: people who feel driven to control. Who are unable to stop, even when their controlling is inappropriate, unrealistic or destructive.

Who have lost control of their need for control.

Okay, I'm in control.
Now how do I get out?

HEART

About addiction:

More people talk about it than understand it.

That's because most people don't know the secret that lies at addiction's heart.

That secret is—surprise—this book's subject.

Because all addicts are control addicts.

And every addiction is an addiction to control.

That's worth repeating:

Every addiction is an addiction to control.

ADDICTS

About addicts:

Addicts are people who can't handle feelings.

Usually because they never learned to as kids. Usually because their parents never taught them. Usually because they couldn't, because *their* parents never taught *them*.

(Usually. There are other paths to addiction, but this is the most common.)

Being unable to handle feelings is a real problem, since feelings tend to keep coming up. So the child of such parents naturally starts looking around for something to make the damn things go away.

Drugs, alcohol, and food are obvious solutions, though anything that alters your mood—work, shopping, sex, porn, TV, videogames, housecleaning, alphabetizing your spice rack—can be turned into an addiction.

And even when they work, these solutions are temporary. Feelings always come back, so a person without some healthier way to handle them is forced to drink, or drug, or eat, or work, or whatever they do to make the feelings go away again.

And that's how an addiction is born.

Some are more destructive than others. But in the end each addiction is the same. Because each has the same goal: *to give the addict control over emotional life.*

And that's why, when asked "What does control have to do with addiction?" I reply, "Everything."

Because finally every addiction is an addiction to control.

The idea of control controls the controllers. We are not in control of the power of control. *~ James Hillman*

CODEPENDENCY

A camel is a horse designed by a committee.

— ALEC ISSIGONIS

Codependency is a camel of a word.

Cobbled together in the 1970s (from "coalcoholic" and "chemical dependency") to describe a cluster of symptoms clinicians were finding in family members of alcoholics, it was later popularized by self-help writers like Melody Beattie.

What does it mean? Good question.

"Codependency" has been defined, but in so many different ways that there is no commonly accepted meaning.

This I discovered while researching a talk I was once asked to give on the subject. I found not one but six definitions of "codependency." Each contained a piece of the truth, and yet none seemed entirely adequate on its own.

So I decided to share all six with my audience.

When I'd finished a man raised his hand and asked, "So what the hell is codependency?"

Everyone laughed.

And then, in a burst of insight, I answered: "Addiction to control."

That has been my working definition of *codependency* ever since.

It's also the best explanation I know for why family members of alcoholics experience the chronic emotional problems they face: guilt, shame, anxiety, depression, dysfunctional relationships, even their own substance abuse.

Here's how it works:

Living with an addict is unpredictable and scary. Inevitably you wish, if only to protect yourself, that you could control their behavior or its consequences.

It's a short step from wishing that to actually trying to do it.

Thus a codependent wife may hide her alcoholic husband's liquor, or pour it down the sink, or lie to his boss about why he's not at work, or to his kids about why he's not home, or to her family about why he never attends birthday parties, or to the neighbors about how she got her black eye.

She may nag, beg, guilt or threaten the alcoholic himself, or try to manage his moods by avoiding conflict, never complaining, never speaking up, never expressing her own thoughts, feelings or needs.

Over time this way of coping becomes second nature to her, a way of handling all experiences, all feelings, and all relationships. It's an approach to living rooted in the belief that survival depends on controlling people, places, and things.

This is the codependent approach.

It affects infects wives, husbands, children, grandchildren, parents, friends, and coworkers of addicts.

But it doesn't end there.

FAMILY

You need not be in relationship with an addict to develop a codependent approach to life.

There are plenty of other ways.

One of the most common is to grow up in a narcissistic family.

Narcissistic families are those unconsciously organized to meet the needs of parents, not children.

This description covers a wide range of possibilities. It includes families that abuse children physically, sexually or emotionally; families fixated on an addicted or mentally ill member; families stressed by poverty, racism, or chronic illness. It includes families where the parents are strict, rigid, and demanding; where parents are not present, physically or emotionally; and those where parents teach children to be seen and not heard.

Kids in narcissistic families have no choice but to adapt to their emotional environment—to protect themselves by trying to control the big people on whom they depend, mainly by pleasing and appeasing them.

Such kids typically experience at least some of the symptoms of codependency: guilt, shame, anxiety, depression. They come to see their own needs and feelings as at best inconvenient, at worst shameful, even dangerous. So at an early age they go into hiding. They become pleasers, appeasers, rescuers and caretakers, better at taking care of others than themselves. And they carry those symptoms into adult life.

And since no family is perfect and no parent is perfectly healthy, every family is at least slightly narcissistic.

Which means nearly all kids grow up at least slightly codependent.

TRAUMA

Another way to create codependency is to traumatize someone.

Trauma ("injured" in Greek) means any shock to mind or body which a person experiences as overwhelming, terrifying, and helpless-making. All traumatic events—whether they occur in a moment (like an assault or a car accident) or extend over time (like war, sexual abuse or chronic illness)—"overwhelm the ordinary systems of care that give people a sense of control, connection and meaning." In other words, central to all trauma is a loss of control.

It is inevitable, then, that all trauma survivors set out in pursuit of the control that they have lost.

Much of this is unconscious and involuntary. The symptoms

of posttraumatic stress disorder—called *re-experiencing, avoidance,* and *hyperarousal*—can all be understood as the mind/body's instinctual attempts to prevent recurrence of the trauma and regain the sense of control that was lost.

Thus the combat veteran hearing a car backfire flashes back to the experience of bombardment and automatically seeks cover. The car crash survivor feels compelled to go miles out of her way rather than drive by the scene of an accident. And the rape victim meeting a man who resembles her assailant reacts with terror, or rage, or both.

What all these survivors have in common is a hypersensitivity to their external environment, which feels like the source of both danger and relief. Preoccupied with people, places, and things they experience as threatening, some spend their lives seeking safety by trying to manage their exposure to those externals.

Most of us already understand this, if only on an intuitive level.

But what many people don't understand is how common—even unavoidable—traumatization is.

"Common occurrences can produce traumatic aftereffects that are just as debilitating as those experienced by veterans of combat or survivors of childhood abuse," writes psychologist Peter Levine, who says such occurrences include

    fetal (intrauterine) trauma, birth trauma, loss of a

parent or close family member, illness, high fever, accidental poisoning, physical injuries (like falls and other accidents), all forms of abuse, abandonment, neglect, witnessing violence, natural disasters (like fires or floods), certain medical and dental procedures, surgery (particularly tonsillectomies with ether), anesthesia, and prolonged immobilization (like the casting or splinting of broken bones).[2]

As a therapist who has treated his share of traumatized clients, I would add: teasing, bullying, public humiliation, academic failure, social awkwardness, sexual embarrassment, getting fired, being the victim of bias, growing up with narcissistic parents, and having an unfaithful spouse.

I'll say more later about compulsive controlling and how to recover from it. Here it's enough to note that:

- More emotional problems are rooted in unresolved trauma than most of us imagine, and

- Anyone trying to understand his or her own compulsive controlling should consider trauma as a possible explanation.

SOCIALIZATION

However common trauma may be, there is another even more inevitable experience that drives human beings into control addiction.

Socialization is that process by which individuals are trained to adapt and conform to their social environment. They do this first by learning—and eventually internalizing—a set of rules, norms, values, behaviors, customs and social skills.

To be socialized is what it means to be *normal*.

And as every human knows, abnormal is dangerous.

That's because we are social beings, wired for life in groups.

Deep within us is the conviction that security comes only with connection, with membership and belonging.

At that same primitive level, we know rejection and expulsion mean isolation and death.

As a result we are driven by social needs only slightly less than by biological ones. Where animals survive by listening to inborn natural instincts, humans survive by managing their relationships with other humans and by obeying the rules imposed by their tribe.

Early sociologists and psychologists generally saw socialization as a good thing, a necessary counterbalance to human selfishness, a civilizing influence.

Most therapists see it differently now.

We see the cost at which people purchase normality:

- How socialization erodes the individual's connection to his or her true self.

- How over time this becomes an inability to even know who that true self is—what one really thinks and feels, wants and needs.

- How self-awareness gets replaced by preoccupation with how other people see them.

- How self-care gets replaced by a compulsion to manage and manipulate other people, places, and things.

- How self-acceptance and self-love are replaced by a craving to feel valued by others.

I see these results daily in clients convinced that happiness lies somewhere Out There, and so spend their lives pursuing external rewards—love, success, approval, popularity, fame, money, possessions—in the belief that such rewards are what life is all about.

Many end up losing themselves.

And, in the process, teach their children to do the same.

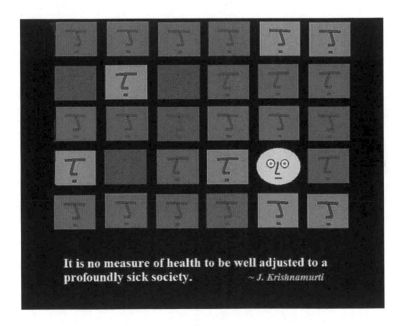

It is no measure of health to be well adjusted to a profoundly sick society.   ~ J. Krishnamurti

CULTURE

There's one more social element that nudges us into compulsive controlling. Let's call it *culture*.

By culture I mean all the unspoken values, rules, assumptions, expectations and preferences of the tribe (or subtribe) to which we belong.

Even within one society, cultures vary wildly. New York bankers live in a world light years away from that of Wisconsin dairy farmers or teens in a Los Angeles barrio. They wear different clothes, speak different languages, dream different dreams, understand the world differently.

But we can't avoid being shaped by some culture, even those

of us who resist it. Culture surrounds us, penetrates our feeling and thinking.

And the culture that saturates us all is a culture of control.

Control, remember, means the ability to tailor reality until it fits our needs and expectations.

Culture is a voice that tells us *what* to need and expect.

It does this indirectly, by promoting some values and dismissing others, rewarding some preferences and denigrating the rest.

For example, take the culture attached to democracy. Who, if they live in a democracy, won't end up expecting and demanding freedom, fairness and equality? Or won't feel outrage when those ideals are violated or ignored?

Or the culture of materialism. Which of us can watch endless ads on TV and not end up wanting to buy stuff and own stuff, new stuff and more stuff, and not feel at least slightly deprived when we can't?

Or the culture of technology. Who hasn't come to depend on electric light, computers, cell phones, laptops, remote controls and microwave ovens to where we panic a little when they break down?

Besides shaping our expectations, all cultures offer one more thing: an unofficial guidebook to getting along by going along.

Do this, culture whispers, *or be different. Conform or be abnormal.*

And as noted in the previous chapter, *abnormal* is dangerous. *Different* is a hard way to live.

Then again, if all you can see is what everyone else sees and all you want is what everyone wants, you're less a member of society than its victim.

Think of culture as socialization in sheep's clothing.

SURVIVAL

All the factors just described—family, trauma, socialization and culture—combine in the human mind to drive controlling behavior.

The ultimate goal of that behavior is the most primitive and stubborn of all human goals: life itself.

I mean here not just physical survival, though certainly much of our controlling (like when we're driving a car or battling an illness) has that as its aim.

I mean emotional, psychological and social survival as well.

We cannot help but believe that control is essential to these, too.

Thus the need to survive emotionally forces children to appease abusive or narcissistic parents, since on the deepest of levels they know they need the security parents represent.

And psychological survival is what demands trauma survivors limit their exposure to threatening triggers, since the alternative is a constant state of fight-or-flight leading to intolerable stress and disintegration of their minds.

And it is social survival that requires each of us to absorb and obey the dictates of the society to which we belong, since— again, on the deepest levels—we know we cannot last long without acceptance by the tribe.

We each believe control is essential to our lives.

This conviction is so unconscious and inescapable that it makes getting control feel like a matter of life and death.

It's why even the idea of losing control produces anxiety, and why control addiction plays like a silent soundtrack behind every human experience.

And where does it come from, this conviction that we must control or die?

Mainly from the structure of our mind.

MONKEYMIND

Monkeymind is a Buddhist metaphor that describes how normal human consciousness operates.

Our minds jump from thought to thought, feeling to feeling, like a monkey leaping from tree to tree to tree.

Unsettled, restless, never content with the present moment, they are constantly distracted by the endless stream of internal chatter passing through.

This is universal.

There are two important things to remember about monkeymind:

1. MONKEYMIND IS, ARGUABLY, INSANE.

That's if we define *sanity* as being in touch with reality. Monkeymind is anything but.

Preoccupied with memories of the past and projections of the future, it spins a narrative saturated with fantasy and only minimal awareness of what's actually happening right here, right now.

Anyone who's tried to meditate knows this narrative all too well. Never have? Try now:

> *Sit still. Close your eyes. Take a deep breath.*

> *Stop thinking. Put all your attention on your breathing instead.*

> *Count your breaths.*

> *(Authorial pause while reader counts.)*

> *How far did you get before your counting was interrupted by a thought?*

That chatter you heard? That's monkeymind.

2. MONKEYMIND IS ALL ABOUT CONTROL.

Acquiring control—editing the reality we have into the one we want—is monkeymind's mission.

It pursues it by recalling old wounds and trying to heal them, anticipating new problems and trying to solve them. (Did you notice, a moment ago, how the thoughts that spontaneously came to mind were wound- or problem-related?) Monkeymind is pain-driven and anxiety-driven, which is why the narrative it spins can feel like a bad horror movie.

It does this with the best of intentions. It's trying to heal us, protect us, make us happy.

Unfortunately the control it chases is an illusion.

So in the end what monkeymind mostly accomplishes is to make us confused, scared, angry, unhappy, and more than a little nuts.

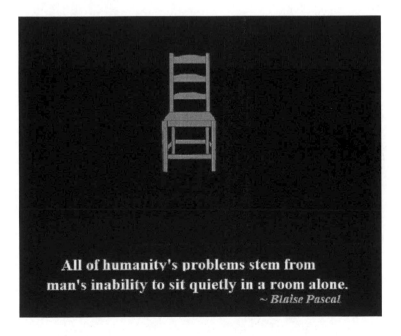

All of humanity's problems stem from man's inability to sit quietly in a room alone.
~ Blaise Pascal

ME AND MY MONKEY

You may have noticed by now that a monkeytrap is not really a trap at all.

It's an invitation to trap yourself.

It succeeds because of a part of the human personality I call the *inner monkey*.

This is the part dominated by monkeymind, the addicted part, the compulsive part. It's the part that grabs on and won't let go.

I once invited my own inner monkey—whom I call Bert—to introduce himself to my blog readers.

Bert

Bert wrote:

I entered Steve's life early, probably well before kindergarten. Probably before he could even talk.

My mission?

To protect him.

From?

Everything.

Scary situations. Painful feelings. Discomfort of every sort.

Rejection. Failure. Disappointment. Frustration. Conflict. Rejection. Sadness.

(Just noticed I listed "rejection" twice. Sorry. I really, really hate rejection.)

I did it mainly by searching relentlessly for ways to change things, things both outside and inside him, to somehow move them closer to what he wanted or needed or preferred.

I also taught him tricks. Coping tricks, like avoiding emotional risks. And relationship tricks, like hiding his feelings and obsessing over how others see him. Even perceptual tricks, like selective memory and imagining I can guess the future or read other people's minds.

None of these works over time. But they gave Steve comfort.

We grew close quickly. I became his constant companion, trusted advisor, and, he thought, very best friend.

I meant well. And at times I've been useful, even helped him out of some bad spots.

But in the end ours has been an unhealthy relationship.

Why?

Because in the end my need for control set Steve at odds with reality instead of teaching him how to accept and coexist and cooperate with it.

It's like that with us inner monkeys.

We mean well. We really do.

But we're also kind of, well, stupid.

For example, some of you already know that the title of this blog refers to a method used in the East to trap monkeys, where fruit is placed in a weighted jar or bottle and the monkey traps himself by grabbing the fruit and refusing to let go.

That's my thing. That's what I do. I grab hold and refuse to let go.

I do this all the time, even when part of me knows it's not working.

One last word:

I'm betting you have one of my brothers or sisters inside you.

You have it as surely as you have fears, and a monkeymind that whispers and worries and scares you.

You may not have noticed this secret tenant before.

But look anyway.

As I said, monkeytraps are just invitations. They work because of what we monkey-driven humans do.

We set traps, then reach into them.

We build cages, then move in and set up housekeeping.

For a description of the traps and cages, read on.

PART II

DYSFUNCTION

A man who fears suffering is already
suffering from what he fears.

— MICHEL DE MONTAIGNE

PLAN A

There's only one reason anyone seeks psychotherapy:

Plan A has broken down.

Plan A is my label for everything we learn as children about life and how to live it.

We each have a Plan A. And we all pretty much learn it in the same place and in the same way.

The place is our family, and the way is unconsciously.

Nobody sits us down at the kitchen table and says, "Listen up. Here's how you do Life." No, they just do Life themselves, and we watch and listen and soak it all up like little sponges.

Which explains why our Plan A tends to look so much like that of our family members.

And it works okay for a while, especially while we're still living in the family. We're all following the same unwritten playbook.

But Plan A always breaks down.

Eventually we move beyond the family into the larger world, filled with new people and new challenges. And we discover that what worked at home doesn't always work out there.

At this point we have, in theory at least, a choice.

We can tell ourselves, "Oh, I see. I guess I need a Plan B."

Or we can tell ourselves, "I must be doing it wrong. I better work harder at Plan A."

Guess which we choose?

Right. Plan A.

Always Plan A.

Two reasons for this. First, we may not even know there's such a thing as Plan B. Childhood trained us to see Plan A as normal. (Why would anyone do Life in any other way?)

Second, even when we suspect there are other options, we

cling to Plan A because it's familiar. We already know how to do it. We can do it in our sleep.

And change is scary.

So we keep following Plan A despite mounting evidence that it no longer works.

And that's when we begin to develop symptoms—anxiety, depression, addictions, communication problems, bad relationships.

It's those symptoms that drive us into therapy.

Seeking, whether we know it or not, a Plan B.

Most people don't enter therapy to change. They're not interested in Plan B.

They want someone to show them how to make Plan A work better.

LESSONS AND RULES

So the first thing to remember about Plan A is that we learn and follow it unconsciously.

And the second thing is that every Plan A has the same goal:

Control over emotional life.

Do this, it tells you, to be safe and avoid pain. Do this to win love and acceptance.

This becomes clearer when you examine the lessons and rules which are Plan A's component parts.

I, for example, grew up in an alcoholic family. Alcoholics are addicts, and as noted earlier, addicts are people who can't handle feelings. So I spend my childhood with people who reacted to my feelings with anxiety, anger, hurt and guilt. And the Plan I evolved (essentially the same Plan evolved by every kid in that situation) reflected all that.

One important lesson: "Feelings are uncomfortable at best, dangerous at worst." This lesson grew into a rule: Feel as little as possible. Think your way through life instead.

Another lesson: "You are responsible for other people's feelings." This grew into a second rule: Never be yourself around other people.

These two lessons were the foundation stones of my Plan A.

They also called my inner monkey into being.

Bert was born to take control of my chaotic emotional life. He set out to accomplish that by doing things like burying feelings, developing an acceptable image, and becoming painfully oversensitive to the emotions, perceptions, and opinions of others.

Interestingly, it was Bert's idea that I become a therapist. Attending to others' feelings while disguising my own seemed a natural fit to my original Plan.

Little did either of us suspect that becoming a healthy therapist would mean I'd have to outgrow Bert and develop a Plan B.

FIVE WEEDS

After the workshop described in chapter 13 (the one where I redefined codependency as control addiction) I went back to doing therapy with clients in the outpatient clinic where I worked.

Mine was still a typical caseload, filled with the same problems every therapist faces.

But now something was different.

Did you ever buy a new car—a new Honda, say—and take it out on the road, and wherever you drove you saw other Hondas? Suddenly the world was filled with Hondas you had never noticed before.

That's what happened to me. Suddenly my caseload was filled with control addicts.

Of course, the clients hadn't changed. I had. It's like I'd put on new eyeglasses. My vision had refocused or sharpened or something, and now I couldn't help seeing how relentlessly and self-destructively controlling they all were.

They? I mean we.

Controlling, I discovered, is a universal addiction. It was everywhere I looked. Not just in clients I'd labeled codependent, but in every client. Not just in clients, but in colleagues and friends and family, and on the nightly news and in whatever I read or watched on TV or in the movies.

And, of course, in myself. (I'd discovered Bert.)

Like a red thread in a carpet, the idea of control snaked through every problem, every motive, every personality, and every life.

Most surprisingly, I noticed that the five most common problems clients brought to therapy all had compulsive controlling in common.

Anxiety, depression, addiction, dysfunctional relationships and problems with parenting all seemed to grow out of the same urge to control what either couldn't or shouldn't be controlled.

Like five different weeds growing out of one root.

THE ANXIOUS

Anxious clients are at once all different and all the same.

Big and little, old and young, rich and poor. Obsessive parents, controlling spouses, insecure employees. Worried seniors, stressed teenagers, scared kids.

Their symptoms are both painful and remarkably common. They can't stop worrying. Their thoughts race. They either can't go to sleep or can't stay there. Their appetite comes and goes. They're self-doubting and perfectionistic. They agonize over mistakes. They get irritable, cranky or tearful. They're self-conscious around other people. Even when alone, with no jobs to do, they can't relax or enjoy themselves.

Some develop physical symptoms: restlessness, muscular tension or pain, teeth grinding, indigestion, nausea, headaches.

Some suffer social anxiety. Others have panic attacks. Still others report obsessive thoughts and/or compulsive behaviors.

But behind all these differences, they have three things in common:

1. THEY TRY TO CONTROL THE FUTURE.

They do this mainly by thinking about it. Anticipating it. Planning it. Worrying about it. Obsessing over it. Forming expectations. In other words, by surrendering their thoughts to the untended mercies of monkeymind.

This highly efficient system keeps anxieties growing like weeds. Because the more the anxious worry about the future, the more anxious they get. And the more anxious they get, the more they worry about the future. And so on.

2. THEY TRY TO CONTROL OTHER PEOPLE.

They do this by insisting—secretly, in the privacy of their monkeyminds—that other people *always* like them, accept them, approve of them, agree with them, admire their clothes, hair, physique, income, intelligence or sense of humor.

They convince themselves that they really *need* other people to do this, and that life will be intolerable when they don't.

As a result they scare the crap out of themselves, and set off on a desperate course of seeking a degree of interpersonal control nobody ever has.

3. THEY OVERCONTROL THEMSELVES.

This habit is an inevitable outgrow of the last. Anxious people try to control other people mainly by editing themselves — hiding the parts they think others won't like.

Most importantly, they bury their feelings instead of expressing them.

That last sentence defines the heart of anxiety.

That's because feelings are — excuse this analogy — like shit.

Like feces, feelings are supposed to be expelled and expressed, not hidden and buried. When they're buried, they don't go away; they collect. The person then becomes emotionally constipated, lives in a constant state of internal self-interruption, pressure, and emotional pain.

Anxiety is the name we give to this pain.

It is not generally recognized that suppression of a feeling makes one afraid of that feeling.

~ *Alexander Lowen*

THE DEPRESSED

For the anxious, constipation is a problem. For the depressed, it's a lifestyle.

Usually it starts unconsciously and in self-defense. All my depressed clients grew up in dangerous families where it was unsafe to be themselves. (See chapter 14.) Kids in such families have little choice but to self-constipate.

Ever been physically constipated? Remember how, the longer it lasted, the more distracted and uncomfortable you felt? How eventually the internal pressure and tension came to sap your energy and occupy all your attention?

That's just what happens to the depressed. It's no accident that people in recovery use excretory metaphors *(my shit's coming up, I can't get my shit together)* to describe emotional processes. Feelings are a kind of waste material, the emotional byproducts of experience, just as feces are physical byproducts of what we eat. And just as physical waste must be expelled from the body, feelings must be expressed—not hidden or stored up. When they aren't we get sick emotionally, physically, and spiritually.

Humans either *express* themselves or *depress* themselves.

The best book I know on all this is Alexander Lowden's *Depression and the Body,* which explains depression as a physical symptom, an exhaustion that comes from fighting oneself by suppressing feelings that need to come out. Lowen writes:

> The self is experienced through self-expression, and the self fades when the avenues of self-expression are closed... The depressed person is imprisoned by unconscious barriers of "shoulds" and "shouldn'ts," which isolate him, limit him, and eventually crush his spirit.[3]

For control addicts—who experience life itself as one long litany of *shoulds* and *shouldn'ts*—some depression is inevitable. And since everyone is addicted to control, it is not surprising that depression is called the common cold of mental illness.

I've had my cold for six decades.

I caught it in grade school. Nobody called it *depression* then. This was the '50s. I'm not sure if back then anyone even knew that kids got depressed.

All I knew was I always felt sad, shy, nervous, worried. Different. Inadequate. Flawed.

I preferred being alone. Preferred books to people. Preferred TV to real life.

"Moody," Mom called me. "Difficult" was Dad's diagnosis.

I also felt bad about feeling bad. *It must be my fault*, I thought. Teachers were always writing on my report cards "could do better if he'd try." So I decided feeling crappy meant I was somehow doing Life wrong, that I'd *feel* better if I just tried harder. I just didn't know how.

I felt this way through high school, college, and into adulthood; through courtship, marriage, and fatherhood; through college, graduate school, and into professional life.

Along the way I got some therapy and some medication and read lots of books. *Lots* of books.

The idea of happiness, always mysterious to me, became a preoccupation, then a challenge, then a quest.

I read everything I could that might cast some light on what had become my life's central question: *How do you feel good about life?*

It was only after I began to work as a therapist that I found an answer.

Doing therapy with control addicts taught me that I hadn't gotten depressed because Dad drank or Mom was unhappy or because they fought or divorced when I was eight. It wasn't because I never had as much money as I wanted or the body I wanted or never wrote the book I always wanted to write, or because of anything that had happened to me.

I was depressed because of how I *reacted* to what happened.

Or rather, didn't react.

We express ourselves, or we depress ourselves.

THE ADDICTED

Everyone I see in therapy is addicted.

So is everyone else I know.

When I first became a therapist I distinguished between addicts and nonaddicts. That distinction no longer makes sense to me.

Now I think we're all addicted to *something*. It's just that some addictions are more obvious than others.

Again (see chapter 12), addicts are people who can't deal with feelings, and so feel compelled to find something that makes feelings going away. This may be a substance (alcohol, drugs, food) or a behavior (work, sex, TV, shopping, video games).

Anything that alters one's mood can be turned into an addiction. That includes behaviors not inherently unhealthy, like exercise or meditation or volunteering.

The variations may be infinite, but they share the same root: the need *to alter or control how one feels.*

My own addictions came in both flavors, substances and behaviors.

When I was a kid my drug of choice was sugar. In grade school I ate it by the spoonful. I also drank maple syrup.

In grad school I graduated to tobacco, furiously smoking a pipe until cumulus clouds formed in my office and my tongue morphed into hamburger.

My compulsive behaviors included watching television (an alternate reality where I spent most of ages 12 through 18), reading books (the alternate reality I still find preferable much of the time), and writing. In my 30s and 40s I carried a spiral notebook everywhere with me, compulsively filling page after page whenever I felt confused or stressed out or scared. There are 31 dusty spirals stacked in a corner of my garage.

And I'm still addicted to work. But I can't write intelligently about that here, since I remain in denial.

These were the main paths I followed into what I call the Garden of Numb.

You know that place. It's where your focus narrows, the world goes away, anxiety recedes, and tension and worry slough off like dirt in the shower.

Great place to visit. Necessary, even. We all need vacations. The world can be a frightening and painful place, and living a human life is no picnic.

The problem comes when you find you can't live outside the Garden.

Each of my addictions eventually took on lives of their own. Each stopped being something I was doing and became something that was doing *me*. I lost control of my need for control.

So now, whenever I meet a new client, I look for two things:

1. What they do, repeatedly and compulsively, to get themselves into the Garden, and

2. How impaired this controlling behavior leaves them.

The symptoms of (2) are pretty predictable:

- *Bad feelings.* Since they have no way but numbness to manage feelings, and since nobody can stay numb constantly, addicts are emotionally uncomfortable much of the time.

- *Bad choices.* Since their unconscious priority is feeling-management, addicts tend to follow the path that is least threatening emotionally, and their decision-making reflects this—instead of, say, an awareness of reality, determination to solve problems, or concern for the needs and feelings of others.

▥ *Bad relationships.* Addicts struggle with relationships simply because they're not all there: their feelings are missing. They can't be fully honest and authentic, can't tolerate honesty and authenticity in others, and can't communicate in a way that promotes real connection and mutual understanding.

See yourself in this?

Don't feel bad.

Remember, we're all control addicts.

If you're human and breathing, there's no avoiding it.

MONKEYSHIPS

I'm a couples therapist who used to be scared of couples.

There's just so much going on in a couples session, so many levels and variables to notice. I was constantly asking myself questions like:

- *What are these people actually saying? What are they holding back?*

- *Which feelings can they express to each other? Which ones do they hide?*

- *Which of their motives are conscious and which are unconscious?*

- *Are they reacting to their current situation or experiencing old feelings from past experiences and unhealed wounds?*

It was a lot of work. Made Bert anxious.

Then things changed for me.

I began studying control, and developed what I call the Monkeyship Theory.

The theory has three tenets:

1. A *monkeyship* is any relationship that turns dysfunctional when the partners try to control each other.

2. All relationships get monkeyish from time to time.

3. Most relationship problems are really control struggles in disguise.

This theory helped me feel safer with couples in two ways.

First, focusing on the idea of control helped me to observe and organize what was happening in sessions, sort of like an Etch-a-Sketch magnet rearranges iron filings. Identifying underlying control issues *(You're rude to my mother / You won't share control of our money / Hold on, she's my daughter, too)* clarified how the couple got into trouble in the first place.

Second, it gave me a way to help them get out of trouble.

I realized my job wasn't so much to fix them or change anything as to help the partners notice what they were already doing—what they tried to control and how they went about it.

I did this mainly by pointing out what I was seeing and hearing.

Mary, you just interrupted John. Does that happen a lot?

John, you look hurt. What's coming up for you right now?

When you apologize, I get the sense that "sorry" is not how you really feel. Am I right?

For many couples, just noticing their patterns and hidden messages helps to defuse tension and redefine conflicts. Once they see what they're doing, they have a choice of whether to keep doing it or not. This alone can feel empowering.

After they learn to spot their own patterns, the next step is to teach them alternatives to control.

There are three, I tell them:

- **Surrender,** which is the ability to stop trying to control what you can't control.

- **Responsibility**, which is the ability to shift your attention from externals (people, places, things) to internals (your own thoughts, feelings, behavior) and to base your choices on what you feel and need.

- **Intimacy**, or the ability to be fully yourself with another person and permit them to do the same with you.

(These are described in more detail in **Part 4: Plan B**.)

Once they understand the alternatives, the job is to get them to practice.

This approach works better with some couples than others. Its success depends mainly on how willing they are to stop playing blame tennis and look hard at themselves.

Those with the courage to do so usually discover that they've been trying to change their partner into the partner they want, instead of accepting the partner they have.

And that, without realizing it, they've been dancing to the toxic theme song of all monkeyships:

Don't be who you are.

Be who I need you to be.

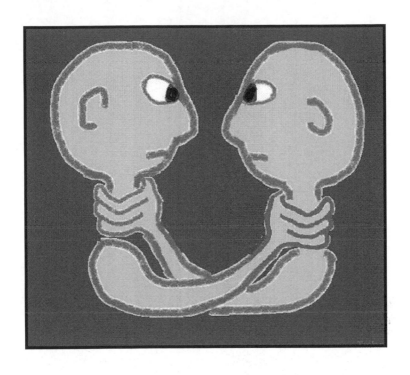

MONKEYPARENTS

I needed clients when I first opened my private practice so I went into local high schools to give talks about parenting.

Everyone's favorite was titled "How to Parent Your Child Through Adolescence Without Committing Murder." Each delivery of this talk generated new clients.

Most, though, weren't parents. They were teenagers, sullen and nervous, dropped off in my waiting room by Mom or Dad with a tag tied to their toe:

Fix my kid.

I jest. Well, partly.

Adolescence brings out the worst in many parents, for a reason which by now should be obvious: it challenges their sense of control.

Before this they could convince themselves they were in charge. *Eat your broccoli,* they'd say, and Junior complied. *It's late, come in now,* and here comes Junior.

Or they could kiss the booboo and give Junior a hug and Junior would stop crying and hug them back. Problem solved.

Then Junior hits puberty and everything changes.

The kid starts acting strangely. Refuses your broccoli; won't even eat your dinner. Comes home late, or not at all. Stops giggling at your jokes. Acts like you're a moron. Rude, defiant, loud, silent, stubborn, irresponsible, self-centered, and incredibly sloppy.

Mom's baby has morphed into an Orc.

This predictable family crisis is called *separation and individuation*. It's a psychological threshold every child needs to cross. When they do they start detaching from their parents, develop their own identity, express their own views and values, and start feeling and functioning like grownups.

All this is essential to a healthy adulthood . Without it, no matter how old or how big someone gets, inside they feel childish and incomplete.

But many parents misunderstand separation and individuation. Even those who do understand usually find it uncomfortable.

And to parents with control issues, it can feel like an earthquake.

Some misread this normal developmental stage as disrespect, disloyalty, rejection, parental incompetence, or a sign their kid no longer loves them.

Some misinterpret it as psychopathology. They start hunting for signs of substance abuse, or Googling *bipolar disorder.*

Some panic. Often these are people for whom parenthood was the one part of life where they felt somewhat in command, could expect to be respected and admired, listened to and obeyed. To such parents a child's defiant *No* can feel like being tossed into deep water without a life preserver.

Some react with hurt, anger, judgment, or withdrawal.

Some try to regain control by imposing new rules, demands or punishments.

Some become emotionally or verbally abusive.

Some become violent.

Some fight with their spouses about it. Some get divorced.

Some get depressed or develop anxiety disorders.

Some drink, drug, or overeat.

And some enter therapy. Where, if they're lucky, they start to learn alternatives to monkeyparenting.

Punish your child when he tells the truth, and he won't make that mistake again.

ME-MONKEYS

Once upon a time there was a handsome young shepherd so self-admiring that he could love nobody else. The gods punished him by making him fall in love with his own reflection in a pond and stare at it until he starved to death.

His name was Narcissus, and every third or fourth day one of his distant cousins shows up in my office.

They're not there for therapy. What they really want is magic. They want someone to teach them how to control the people in their lives. They usually experience other people as unappreciative, ungrateful and ungiving, and they want me to teach them how to get those other people to love them better.

They're my toughest clients.

Most people mistake narcissism for vanity or self-love.

It's not. It's the opposite.

Narcissists are hungry blind people.

Usually they're hungry because they didn't get fed emotionally as kids. Most grew up in dysfunctional families unable to provide adequate attention, acceptance, approval or affection, the four emotional staples known as *narcissistic supplies.*

They're blind because they carry that hunger into adulthood, where they are so preoccupied with getting fed that they ignore the needs and feelings of the people around them.

I explain it this way to clients:

> *Narcissism is like trying to drive a car that has a mirror instead of a windshield. You look out over the dashboard and you don't see streets or traffic or pedestrians; you see only your own preferences, your own feelings and needs. You're so preoccupied with those things that you don't see where you're going. You don't see who you're running over to get there. And when you do, you barely notice the bump.*

Narcissists come in many disguises, some easier to spot than others. The most obvious are the *showmen*—loud, demanding, self-conscious Donald Trump types who constantly polish their image, impose their point of view, and leave me feeling less like a therapist than an audience.

Then there are the *victims*, eager to tell me their tales of abuse and betrayal, and desperate that I confirm that none of it was their fault.

Then the *addicts*, so busy struggling with their tangled, unmanageable feelings that they're simply unavailable for healthy relationship with anyone else.

Finally the *codependents*, who appear to be forever putting everyone else first, but whose caretaking, people-pleasing and conflict avoidance are actually subterfuges meant to protect them from rejection and win a few emotional table scraps in return.

As I said, my toughest clients.

Two reasons for this:

The first reason is that they're secretly terrified. The emotional starvation they suffered as kids left them convinced there was something wrong with them, and they've carried that belief ever since. The false self they construct and show the world—be it codependent or Trumpesque—was built to hide their secret shame, sense of incompleteness, and conviction they're unlovable. It's hard to do therapy with them because therapy requires trust and many trust no one. (How can you trust others if you can't trust your parents? Or can't trust yourself?) Many are simply too frightened to come out of hiding and reveal the person inside. Some have hidden behind their false front for so long they can no longer distinguish it from their real self.

The second reason: I'm a me-monkey myself.

I mentioned earlier that it was Bert's idea I become a therapist. A nifty way, he thought, to put my codependent Plan A to work. I would help others solve their problems, win narcissistic supplies in return, and get my emotional needs met without having to reveal either my needs or my emotions.

That was decades ago. I'm well into my Plan B now. But every Plan B is an ongoing project, and I still have to work at mine.

There are days when my needs collide with my clients'. Some days I'm tired and cranky, and they need patience and acceptance. Other days I need reassurance that I'm a good therapist, and they need to express dissatisfaction or anger. I expect it will always be thus.

Carl Jung:

> We cannot change anything unless we accept it. Condemnation does not liberate, it oppresses...If a doctor wishes to help a human being he must be able to accept him as he is. And he can do this in reality only when he has already seen and accepted himself as he is. Perhaps this sounds very simple, but simple things are always the most difficult. In actual life it requires the greatest art to be simple, and so acceptance of oneself is...the acid test of one's whole outlook on life.[4]

We teach what we want to learn.

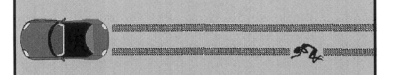

A narcissist is like the driver of a car that has a mirror instead of a windshield. When he looks out over the dashboard he sees only himself. He doesn't see the street, or the other cars. He doesn't see pedestrians. He doesn't even notice when he runs over them.

DEFENSE DEPARTMENT

Defenses (or *defense mechanisms* or *ego defenses*) are psychological processes meant to reduce anxiety.

Originally conceived by Freud as strategies employed by the mind to manage unacceptable impulses, defenses are automatic, unconscious, universal, and essentially inevitable.

To be human is to be defensive.

Our defenses get triggered when we face something painful or frightening, and they rely heavily on denial and distortion to make emotional life manageable.

What do defenses have to do with control?

Just this:

The idea of control itself—the idea that we can edit reality to our personal specifications and so avoid emotional pain—is the mother of all defenses.

Real control is possible and appropriate sometimes. But we attempt it in so many situations where it's clearly impossible or inappropriate that it's hard not to see our controlling as rooted in denial, distortion and self-delusion.

Any defense can be functional or dysfunctional. It's functional when it helps us to get our needs met, and dysfunctional when it distorts reality in ways that impair effective functioning. That's why so many therapies try to help clients become more aware of the defenses they employ, and make better choices about which ones to utilize and which ones to minimize.

I do the same with my clients.

The next five chapters describe the defenses I find myself addressing most often in therapy.

INTERRUPTIONS

The defenses I see most often are *suppression* and *repression*.

The first is the conscious choice to conceal thoughts or feelings. Say you hurt my feelings, I get angry and decide you're an insensitive jerk. But I'm also scared that if you know this you'll get mad and hurt me again. So I hide both my anger and my opinion from you.

That's *suppression*.

Then again, say you're an important person to me—my parent, my spouse or my boss—and the idea of your hurting or rejecting me is seriously scary. So scary that I worry my thoughts and feelings may leak out accidentally. So I defend against that possibility by hiding them even from myself. I bury them in my unconscious, essentially forgetting what I think and feel.

That's *repression*.

For socialized humans suppression and repression are the cost of doing business. There's no other way to coexist with other humans than by interrupting our own feelings. (Imagine a world in which everyone expressed *all* their feelings *all* the time.)

So these are necessary, largely functional defenses. Carefully taught in both schools *(No talking, people)* and families *(Don't cry or I'll give you something to cry about)*, they're also encouraged by society at large. Notice how many movie heroes and heroines are emotionally *un*expressive—strong, silent, stoic, cool.

Which leads most of us to overlook how dangerous these defenses can be as well.

I've already described how chronically stuffing feelings damages us emotionally, causing anxiety, depression and addiction. But overdependence on suppression and repression also damages:

▨ *Relationships.* A healthy relationship is one which addresses and meets the emotional needs of both partners. That's impossible when partners regularly hide how they really feel.

▨ *Communication.* Couples unable to share feelings usually

argue about the wrong things. Emotional messages get disguised as fights about money or relatives or parenting, when what the partners really need to ask are questions like *Do you really love me? Do you accept me as I am? Can I trust you? Will you be here tomorrow?*

- *Intimacy.* Intimacy means being myself with you and allowing you to do the same with me. But being myself means being my feelings at least some of the time. I once knew a pair of bright, traumatized people so frightened of feelings that they tried to achieve a purely intellectual intimacy, talking endlessly of ideas and theories. It sounded sad, like two computers trying to converse. We are more than our minds.

- *Parenting.* One of the most important things kids learn from their parents is how to identify and express feelings. But parents who pretend they don't *have* feelings produce kids who are essentially unprepared to handle adult life. Expecting such kids to succeed is like sending them out to travel the expressway without first teaching them how to drive.

- *Physical health.* Feelings live in the body, so expressing them fully means expressing them physically. We're wired to strike out when angry, flee when frightened, and cry when sad. (Kids do all this naturally, which is why, until we start training them out of it, most kids are emotionally healthier than adults.) To interrupt these natural methods of purging our feelings requires that we tense the muscles we would use to express them. We do this unconsciously and chronically. Then we wonder why we're always tired or suffer chronic pain or tension in our neck, back, head, or stomach. One of my clients was chief of family medicine at a local hospital and I asked him what being a doctor had taught him about people. "That there's no such thing as a purely physical illness," he replied. We suppress and repress our way into ill health.

▣ *Self-awareness.* A surprising number of clients can't answer simple questions about themselves. *What do you like? What do you love? What do you want?* Then again, not so surprising, given all of the above. Sidney Jourard writes, "No man can come to know himself except as an outcome of disclosing himself to another person."[5]

The more you run away from something, the more you run into it.

MISTAKEN IDENTITIES

I'm six years old and my father is a tall, red-headed man with a deep voice who beats me with a belt every day.

Now imagine it's thirty years later. Dad's dead and gone, I'm fully grown, and I have a job interview. The interviewer is a tall, red-headed man with a deep voice. Guess how I feel when I first shake his hand?

That's *transference.*

Transference is what happens when one relationship feels like another. Freud, who discovered transference in his patients' emotional responses to him, never called it a defense, though clearly its main function is defensive. It kicks in when the mind finds a danger signal in its vicinity, some red flag (like my interviewer's red hair) that reminds us of some prior danger or trauma. In that moment the person reacts emotionally as if the old danger has returned.

Transference can be puzzling *(Why do I hate this man I just met?)*, but it's not inherently pathological. It becomes a problem only when it leads us into maladaptive thoughts, feelings, or behavior (like punching redheaded strangers in the mouth).

Transference comes up all the time in therapy, where clients commonly mistake therapists for their parents. Some analytic therapists define the goal of therapy as working through this transference, getting a patient to where he or she feels like an adult in the presence of this authority figure. In my work, this means helping clients get to where they no longer feel the need to control my reactions, where they feel safe enough to relax and be fully themselves.

Another popular form of mistaken identity is summarized in a joke:

> *Dad's boss yells at him. Dad comes home and yells at Mom. Mom yells at Big Sister. Big Sister yells at Little Brother. Little Brother kicks the dog. Dog pees on the rug.*

This is *displacement*: the transfer of aggressive feelings from the person who hurt you to a safer target.

> *I'm a grad student interning at a day treatment program for patients with severe mental illness. On the first day, my supervisor shows me around. When we walk through the cafeteria, a*

young man suddenly stands up, overturns his chair, and tries to punch me. Later, my supervisor explains that I resemble the father who'd raped this young man when he was five. How much of his reaction was transference, how much displacement? I don't know. But it was clearly mistaken identity. I'm not who the young man needed to punch.

Finally, there's a kind of displacement that occurs when the safer target we choose is ourselves.

In this case, Dad doesn't yell at Mom; instead, he turns his anger against himself. He feels guilty, inadequate, depressed, and even suicidal. Gestaltists call this mistaken identity *retroflection*—when you do to yourself what you want to do to someone else.

Retroflection is common among depressed clients as well as those plagued by chronic guilt. They often don't believe me when I suggest it's not really themselves they're angry at. But if I can get them to redirect some of their anger outward (*I really do hate my husband* or *I guess Mom really is a bitch*), the guilt begins to lift.

SUPERPOWERS

No, I can't read your mind.

No, I can't predict the future.

No, that doesn't stop me from trying.

Welcome to the wonderful world of *projection*.

The classic definition of projection is *the unconscious misattribution of unwanted parts of the self onto others*. This can apply to qualities, thoughts, or feelings.

> *Say I think I'm fat. You and I meet for the first time. My first thought as we shake hands is* I bet she thinks I'm fat. *Projection.*

Or say I really dislike you. It's a short step from there to imagining that you dislike me. Projection.

I think of projection as amateur mindreading, because that's how it tends to appear in therapy.

A group member who's habitually late comes in 15 minutes after group has started. She sits down, looks around at the other members, and finds a woman who's frowning. "Go ahead, say it," she blurts. "I'm late again. I'm selfish, I'm disruptive, you all hate me, and I should drop out of group. Say it." "Actually," the frowner replies, "I just realized I have to pee."

Another common form of projection is fortunetelling. That's where we project our thoughts—our fears, mainly—onto the future, and end up convinced that we know what's going to happen. We *know* we'll fail that test, blow the audition, lose the argument. We just know.

A young man with low self-esteem goes to ask his girlfriend's father for permission to marry his daughter. Driving over he is tortured by fears that Dad will find him unsuitable and his request will be denied. By the time he reaches the house he's begun to resent this imagined rejection. He walks up to the older man and says: "Go to hell. I wouldn't marry her if you paid me." Projection.

The two examples above illustrate the sorts of problems projection can cause. Projection blurs our boundaries to where we confuse an internal problem (here, anxiety) with an external one (actual judgment or rejection by Dad). Then we act as if our feeling was triggered by something external and real, not by something internal and imagined. We end up reacting to something that hasn't happened.

People who rely too heavily on their superpowers tend to live lives beset by imaginary enemies and crises, fighting unnecessary battles both in their heads and out in the world.

OSTRICH

A man out walking one night finds his neighbor on hands and knees under a street lamp. "What's wrong?" he asks. "I lost my house key," moans the neighbor. So the man gets down beside the neighbor and together they search the street, without success. Finally the man asks, "Where were you when you lost the key?" "In the house," the neighbor replies. "In the house? Then why are we searching for it out here?" "Oh, it's light out here," replies the neighbor. "It's dark in the house."

The defense called *denial* is about avoiding dark places. It means refusing to acknowledge an unpleasant reality we're afraid could overwhelm us.

Denial is the most common defense mechanism because it underlies so many of the others. *Suppression* and *repression* deny the existence of troublesome feelings, *intellectualization* tries to bypass feelings entirely, *projection* denies our inability to know the unknowable, and so on.

Like other defenses, denial can be adaptive or maladaptive. Some of it—like denying the inevitability of our own death or the risks of driving on highways or eating in restaurants—is essential to daily functioning.

I think of this as *small-d denial*, as opposed to *large-D Denial*, which is pathological.

Large-D Denial is familiar to anyone who's ever known an active alcoholic or drug addict or grown up in a family with an addict at its emotional center.

> *Once I refused to get into the car, telling my Dad he was drunk and I wasn't going anywhere with him. He hit me and shoved me in the car. My mother cried and told me never to criticize my father's drinking. How could I spoil such a nice family outing?*

This is the famous elephant-in-the-living-room syndrome, where everyone in the family ignores something that's painfully obvious to outsiders.

Another form is what Alcoholics Anonymous calls *stinking thinking*, the denial-ridden thought process of alcoholics:

> *I'm a social drinker. I can stop whenever I like. It's only one beer. I deserve to relax. If you were different I wouldn't need to drink.*

Everyone's against me. Life's just too hard for me. Who cares? You have to die someday.

Control addiction, too, could not exist without denial, since it allows us to forget the mountain of prior experience reminding us how limited our ability to control reality is.

Control addicts, too, employ stinking thinking. It takes various forms, but behind them all is one dangerous (and often unconscious) assumption:

If I just try again or harder or longer, or differently, I can finally make things turn out the way I want them to.

Two other forms of denial that crop up in therapy are blaming and victimization.

Clients *blame* when they don't want to take responsibility for problems. It's the path of least resistance and greatest comfort. And given the normal vicissitudes of life and relationships, there's never a shortage of people, places, or things to blame.

Dad was a drunk. Mom was depressed. My parents fought all the time. My brother was a bully. My sister never stopped complaining. Mom and Dad loved X best. We never had enough money. I was sick a lot. I grew up in a shitty neighborhood. My teachers didn't like me. What chance did I have?

Victimization is a more unconscious and complicated form of blaming. It's what happens when a person becomes defined by prior painful experiences.

Victims often start out denying that they're victims. Sometimes their memories are too painful to bear, and sometimes they've been trained (e.g., by someone who abused them) to see themselves as responsible for whatever bad thing happened. The work with such victims is to help them enter the dark house and face the pain hidden there.

Other victims can't get out of the house. They live in a kind of waking nightmare: the bad thing that happened to them doesn't feel like it's over and done with. They carry it around with them in their bodies and their mind, and it reshapes them the way the artist's wire reshapes a bonsai tree. It colors their view of themselves, other people, life itself. For them there is no present or future, only a past that recurs endlessly.

The goal of therapy with these people is to help them escape the dark house, redefine themselves as adults responsible for their lives, and develop the power to love, protect, and take care of themselves.

The truth is like
a bear in your house.

You can run from it.

You can hide.

You can do this for years.

You just can't escape.

GUMCHEWING

Ever chew gum for too long?

Until it's a flavorless wad, your jaws are weary, and you wonder: "Why is this junk still in my mouth?"

We do this all the time with our minds.

We chew the same thoughts over and over and over. We give this habit different names: *worrying, obsessing, perseveration.*

They all amount to the same thing—a kind of futile mental gumchewing.

They're not defenses, strictly speaking, but these habits of mind clearly serve a defensive function.

They're one of monkeymind's favorite ways of trying to control feelings.

Think about this long enough, monkeymind whispers, *and you'll figure things out, and then you'll feel better.*

But you don't.

You don't figure things out; you just keep chewing endlessly.

And you don't feel better, you feel worse.

That's because mental gumchewing is not analysis (which leads to clarity) or problem-solving (which produces solutions) or planning (which fosters discipline) or even venting (which discharges feelings and brings emotional relief).

It's not even *thinking*, if we define thinking as using your mind to consider something carefully.

Gumchewing isn't using your mind; it's allowing your mind *to use you.*

It's unconscious, automatic and mindless. It's also dysfunctional, which means it won't do you any good at all.

And the harm it does is considerable. It can create anxiety and depression where neither existed before, by keeping your attention focused mainly on problems and pain.

Where you put your attention is what gets nurtured, someone once said. Gumchewing keeps inflating pain and problems until you can't think of anything else.

It's like scratching an itch and making it worse.

Or like picking through garbage expecting to find a diamond.

JUST THE WORLD

I never really wanted those grapes anyway. I am sure they are sour.

— AESOP

Rationalization means explaining something is a way that is comforting but dishonest.

Control addicts use rationalization all the time. They actually have to, in order to convince themselves that control is essential and possible.

Sometimes it appears as *stinking thinking*, the form described in the last chapter (*If I just try a little harder, a little longer...*).

Sometimes it manifests as mistaking the desirable for the possible, a type of thinking I call *the shoulds*.

He should take better care of me emotionally. He should know what I feel and give me what I need. He should know when I need a hug or to be listened to or to be left alone. He should know what I want in bed. When I'm upset he should know what to say to make me feel better. If he really loved, me he'd just know.

The *shoulds* can transform a reasonable desire *(I want X)* to an unrealistic expectation *(I should have X)* and, ultimately, to an emotional problem *(I'm angry that I don't have X)*.

Control addicts regularly apply this kind of wishful thinking to other people, places, things, and themselves. Perfectionists *should* on themselves constantly.

I should be thinner, richer, and smarter. I should be further along in my career. I should be nicer to my mother. I should be a better parent. I shouldn't get so angry. I shouldn't have made that mistake. I shouldn't make any mistakes. I can't stand mistakes.

A third form of rationalization is rooted in the following belief:

Good things happen to good people; bad things happen to bad people.

This is called the *Just World Hypothesis*, and most people believe in it whether they realize it or not.

It explains why we tend to feel guilty when bad things happen to us and why we torture ourselves with second-guessing (*If only I hadn't X*). It's common among religious people, raised on the idea of sin. But belief in God is no prerequisite to belief in a Just World. I once worked with an atheist who argued endlessly against the existence of God, but never doubted, when confronting personal misfortune, that he himself had somehow caused it.

Why do we cling to this bias? It provides the illusion of control.

If bad things can happen to good people, that means everyone's at risk. But if the good are rewarded and the guilty punished, maybe I can avoid punishment by being good, and maybe the world makes some sort of sense.

Belief in a Just World also leads to even more pernicious misinterpretations, like blaming the victim.

> *She was kidnapped at knife-point from a restaurant parking lot by a drifter who raped her twice. But the jury showed little sympathy, and the rapist was acquitted. "We all feel she asked for it by the way she was dressed," said the foreman.*

The type of victim-blaming I hear most often in therapy is *self-blame*, where clients impede their own recovery by taking unrealistic responsibility for bad things that happen to them. It's common among abuse survivors and people who grew up in families prone to unpredictability and emotional turmoil, where kids often got blamed for things that weren't their fault. They were left feeling vulnerable vaguely guilty, and too quick to blame themselves.

Sure, imagining cause-and-effect relationships where they don't exist can be comforting.

But ours isn't a Just World or the world we want and maybe not even the world we deserve.

Just the world we have.

Most people believe in the Just World Hypothesis, which holds that we get what we deserve.

It's why we feel guilty when misfortune befalls us.

But it's not a just world.

And bad things happen to good people all the time.

ON THIS BUS

"The healthiest anyone ever gets is neurotic."

Thus spoke my first supervisor. I was dismayed. Back then, both as a new therapist and a recovering depressive, I clung to the idea of mental healthiness the way a sinner clings to the idea of redemption.

Decades later I know my supervisor was right.

Neurotic means split into two parts: one public, one private. You create neurosis by convincing a person that it is neither acceptable nor safe to be himself or herself.

This happens to everyone. It is the inevitable result of

socialization and other forms of conditioning which teach us not to be who we are .

Think of it as what happens when two sets of needs collide.

We each need to function as autonomous individuals, to operate in ways that meet our individual needs. Some needs are physical (food, shelter, etc.), some psychological, some emotional. We have a psychological need to establish ourselves as unique individuals, for example (see the discussion of separation and individuation in chapter 28), and an emotional need to express how we feel (see chapters 24 and 25 on anxiety and depression). Call these the *self-needs*.

At the same time, we're also social animals with *social needs*. We need contact and connection with other people, need their acceptance, approval, affection, protection, and support. No less than the self-needs, these social needs define what it means to be a human being.

But getting social needs met can be costly. Even if we grow up in a reasonably healthy family able to love and accept us unconditionally, the world outside is less gentle. There we face inevitable demands to adapt and conform, to redefine and disguise ourselves according to what the tribe expects. And we have no choice but to comply.

When I work with couples I explain that all relationships are difficult because they force us to wrestle endlessly with two questions:

How can I have you without losing me?

And how can I have me without losing you?

Every socialized human being struggles with the same questions. How can we satisfy self-needs and social needs at the same time? How can we belong to the larger tribe without losing what makes us unique individuals?

So pervasive is this struggle that it can blur the boundaries that define us. For many it becomes hard to tell where we end and the rest of the world begins.

> *I'm mad at Dad. But if Dad knows I'm angry he may reject me, and that scares me. I'm afraid it would leave me feeling hurt, guilty, inadequate, abandoned, and/or disinherited. So I hide my anger in self-defense.*

> *Am I controlling myself in order to control Dad? Or am I controlling Dad in order to control myself?*

Thus I get split into two selves, private and public, real-me and false-me, controller and controlled.

And my boundary gets blurred, and after a while I can't tell who I really am, what I really need, or how I really feel.

Again, nobody can avoid the tension between self and environment. So this happens to all of us.

It's normal to end up scared, neurotic, and trapped by the control addiction to which neurosis gives birth.

In other words:

We're all monkeys on this bus.

MONKEYTRAPPED

Earlier I described how they trap monkeys in Asia by placing bait in a heavy jar with a narrow neck. The monkey smells the bait, reaches in to grab it, and traps himself by refusing to let go.

The traps to which humans are vulnerable are *psychological* monkeytraps: situations that trigger us into holding on when we really should let go.

How can you tell when you're at risk of entrapment?

Three tips:

1. NOTICE WHERE YOU'RE UNCOMFORTABLE.

We're controlling whenever we need or want to change some piece of reality instead of accepting it or adapting to it as is. And we're most likely to want to change those realities that make us uncomfortable. So inevitably it's our discomfort zones where we're most likely to get monkeytrapped.

> Bert: *Personally, I hate rejection, so I'm most controlling with people I think might reject me. I hide feelings I think will upset them, pretend to agree when I really don't, avoid confronting behavior I dislike, laugh at stupid jokes, and so on and so on. It keeps me busy.*

2. NOTICE WHERE YOU'RE STUCK.

Stuck as in not learning, healing, or growing—struggling with the same problem over and over. You know you're monkey-trapped whenever you find yourself doing what you already know doesn't work but you can't think of an alternative.

> Bert: *All that controlling I just described traps me because it (a) stops me from being myself, which (b) prevents me from ever getting accepted as myself, which (c) keeps me scared of rejection, which brings me right back to (a). It's like riding an endless merry-go-round.*

3. NOTICE WHERE YOU'RE SCARED.

Like all addictions, compulsive controlling is anxiety-driven. We stay monkeytrapped because we're scared to do anything else. Sometimes even the thought of giving up control in such situations is enough to raise our anxiety. And often we forget (if we ever knew) that alternatives to controlling even exist.

> *Bert: It took me decades to see that controlling doesn't work. Or that it does, but only for ten minutes at a time. Then another scary thing comes along and I have to control that. And life being what it is, there's no end to scary things. So as an anxiety-reduction tactic, controlling is a total flop. It still takes effort to remind myself that detaching is an option and that I can reduce my anxiety by talking about feelings instead of acting them out.*

I tell clients who can't remember these three tips to at least remember this:

Scared people are the most controlling people.

And controlling people are the ones who remain the most scared.

HAMMER

When the only tool you have is a hammer, every problem starts to look like a nail.

— ABRAHAM MASLOW

Occasionally a client gets discouraged about escaping control addiction.

This may happen after we've spent hours discussing their narcissistic family, their abuse as children, the ravages of socialization, or how inevitably we all get neurotically split.

"What's the point?" they may say. "If all these factors push us into compulsive controlling, and everyone ends up addicted to control, what hope is there for me?"

It's at this point I give my little talk about problem redefinition:

There are two ways to see any problem. We can define it as the situation we're facing, or we can define it as our response to that situation. Often there's not much we can do about the first. But there's a lot we can do about the second.

Control is the only tool most people have.

It's essential in some situations, of doubtful use in others, and sometimes it's downright destructive.

The job of the recovering control addict is not to give up all controlling—that's impossible—but to learn when to use the hammer and when to put it down and seek alternatives.

Or put another way, recovery is the process of learning to distinguish control from *dyscontrol*—controlling that is compulsive, destructive, and/or counterproductive.

Key to this distinction is a deep understanding of the real reasons we seek control. Which is the subject of the next section of this book, **Emotion.**

Life is a patient teacher. It doesn't mind repeating the lesson until you learn it.

PART III

EMOTION

It is not easy to deal scientifically with feelings.

— SIGMUND FREUD

PIVOT

In this book's introduction I mentioned the Four Laws of Control.

Again, the First Law was

We are all addicted to control.

And the Second was

This addiction causes most (maybe all) of our emotional problems.

We come now to the Third Law:

Behind this addiction stands the wish to control feelings.

This is an important but difficult law, especially for anyone trying to recover from control addiction.

It is difficult because it requires us to make a sort of psychological pivot, a reframing of our emotional experience, what it means, and how to handle it.

It's important because those of us who can learn this law have a chance of recovering.

And those who can't, don't.

We do not see things as they are.

We see things as we are.
~ Anaïs Nin

THE THIRD LAW

This Third Law defines the real—though largely unconscious—goal of all controlling behavior: to control *how we feel*.

Here *feel* refers to two types of experiences, physical and emotional.

What human beings want most is to avoid uncomfortable versions of both.

This is so obvious as to not need stating. It would be easy for anyone reading this to list any number of physical experiences they'd rather avoid, ranging from the minor (stubbed toes and bug bites) to the more problematic (sunburn, broken bones, dehydration) to the potentially fatal (assault, starvation, hypothermia).

Similarly, it's not hard to think of emotional experiences you'd rather do without, from the mild (like minor annoyances and frustrations) to the more painful (conflict, rejection, disappointment) to the emotionally crippling (anxiety attacks, suicidal depression, paralyzing grief).

We spend our lives navigating around and away from such experiences.

Most of the time we don't think about it the way you don't have to think about not petting a bumble bee. Avoidance of discomfort flows naturally from the survival instinct built into us.

In fact the human urge to control externals—people, places, and things—probably originated as a reaction to all sorts of physical discomforts and dangers.

> Hey, it's raining. Let's duck into this cave. Hey, let's run away from that angry bear.

But then something happened.

We evolved. Our big brains developed. We became skilled at imagining and anticipating, which in turn led to planning and worrying. (See chapter 19.)

We evolved from animals reliant on natural instinct into the animal that worries, who spends its life trying to avoid discomfort in all its forms, including emotional ones.

Especially those.

Hey. Let's not feel mad, sad, or scared. Let's arrange life so as to avoid whatever makes us feel those ways. And let's also avoid frustration, rejection, hurt, disappointment, confusion, and embarrassment.

This became our priority, our default position as a species.

And that's where we drifted into trouble. Because to take this position is to ignore the function of feelings.

FEELINGS

We socialized human beings are so busy managing our feelings that we forget (if we ever knew) why we have them in the first place.

Why *do* we have feelings?

More specifically, what is the purpose of emotional reactions?

There are actually several. But the one most relevant here is: information.

Feelings *tell us something about what we're experiencing.*

Usually something important.

This function is clear enough on the physical level, where your empty stomach tells you when to eat, a full bladder tells you when to pee, and the sting in your finger tells you when to pull back from a flame.

Similarly, emotional responses inform us when we're being hurt (we get mad), suffering a loss (sad), facing some danger (scared), or are successfully getting our needs met (glad).

As I said, important information.

Psychiatrist David Viscott:

Our feelings are our sixth sense, the sense that interprets, arranges, directs and summarizes the other five. Feelings tell us whether what we experience is threatening, painful, sad or joyous...Not to be aware of one's feelings, not to understand them or know how to use or express them, is worse than being blind, deaf or paralyzed.[6]

Feelings are like the radar a pilot uses to orient himself when flying at night. How else, in all that darkness, can he know where he is or what he's flying into?

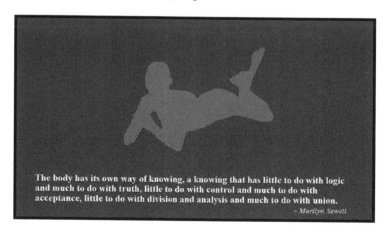

The body has its own way of knowing, a knowing that has little to do with logic and much to do with truth, little to do with control and much to do with acceptance, little to do with division and analysis and much to do with union.
~ Marilyn Sewell

RADARLESS

On the other hand, what happens when our radar gets disabled?

We're left blind and bewildered.

> Feelings are our reaction to what we perceive, and in turn they color and define our perception of the world. Feelings, in fact, *are* the world we live in. Because so much of what we know depends upon our feelings, to be awash in confusing or dimly perceived feelings is to be overwhelmed by a confusing world.[7]

Which may explain why so many people seek therapy.

In Part 2 we discussed common ways in which emotional

radar gets suppressed or damaged. You may have grown up in a dysfunctional family where, to avoid rejection, you learned to smother your emotional self. Abuse or some other trauma may have left you chronically anxious and hypervigilant, unable to clearly distinguish your present reality from your past. Socialization may have pulled your attention away from your own needs and feelings to the expectations of parents, teachers, family and friends. Cultural pressure and the need to belong may have smothered your individuality. And monkeymind may have so distracted you with its incessant chatter that you lost touch with your body and along with it the ability to answer the simple question *How do I feel?*

This happens to all of us. It is normal for socialized individuals to lose touch with the river of feelings flowing inside them.

Normal, and a problem. Because without access to our emotional radar, we cannot adequately:

- Defend ourselves against danger,

- Identify what we need,

- Know who we are,

- Connect meaningfully with others, or

- Feel fully alive.

PAIN

First, consider the usefulness of pain.

This usefulness is obvious on the physical level. Physical pain exists to warn us against dangers to our physical body. How else would we learn not to touch hot stoves or pet bumble bees?

In our pursuit of comfort we often forget how necessary pain is. But even a brief glimpse into a life where this sort of radar has gone missing is a peek into horror. I recall reading about a little girl whose leprosy led to permanent loss of sensation in her extremities, and who used to bite off her fingertips so she could paint with her own blood.[8]

Emotional pain is no less essential. Again, its function is to tell us something important about what we are experiencing. We ignore that information at our peril.

One way I learned this was by sitting with clients after their divorces or breakups and reviewing all the red flags they'd ignored during the relationship.

I always felt lonely in the marriage.
I was constantly walking on eggshells.
Everything was always my fault.
He drank a lot, but I told myself that would change.
I felt her pulling away from me, but it seemed safer not to talk about it.

Each of these people admitted that their radar had tried to warn them of the storm ahead. But hindsight is usually 20/20. Foresight is much less expensive. But we need to use our emotional radar to access the foresight with which we are naturally endowed.

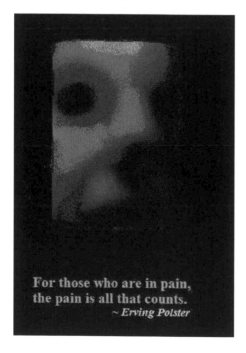

For those who are in pain,
the pain is all that counts.
~ *Erving Polster*

NEEDS

We also need emotional radar to tell us what we need.

You walk into a party, a crowded room filled with sights, sounds and people. What do you notice first? If you're hungry, you notice the buffet. If you're thirsty, you notice the open bar. If you're a thirsty alcoholic, you notice the booze. If you have to pee, you notice the bathroom. If your leg is broken, you notice the nearest empty seat. If you're shy, you notice the friendliest face, or perhaps the room's most private corner.

Psychologists call this selection process *figure/ground formation. Figure* refers to whatever leaps out at us and pulls our attention away from the cluttered background. It is figural because it addresses our most important or most pressing need.

Anyone who's ever had a toothache drive everything else out of their awareness knows what I mean.

Healthy individuals allow figure/ground formation to guide them when making choices and solving problems. They listen for instructions—pay attention to what they're feeling, sensing, and noticing—and respect and rely on what they hear.

Neurotic individuals, on the other hand, are bad listeners. Caught in a war between their self-needs and their social needs (see chapter 37), they get fragmented, split into two parts—public and private, false-self and real-self, controller and controlled. This leads them into ignoring the instructions their feelings send them. In their hunger to belong or win approval they may overwork, neglect their physical health, marry the wrong person, enter the wrong career, smother their creativity, stifle their expressiveness, embrace the wrong values, and spend their lives at war with themselves.

Living this way is like taping over the "check engine" light on your dashboard, the one that's telling you to peek under the hood.

"For the individual to satisfy his needs, he must be able to *sense* what he needs," Fritz Perls wrote.[9]

If you can't sense what you need, how can you take care of yourself?

And if you can't take care of yourself, how can you ever be happy?

IDENTITY

Another important question: If you don't know how you feel, how can you know who you are?

Many clients enter therapy saying they're unhappy. Usually they can't explain why. Since I define *happy* as the emotional state that accompanies getting your needs met, my first question to them is usually: "What do you want?"

And they often reply: "I don't know."

This is a clear symptom of control addiction. Usually these are people distracted by externals, caught up in trying to manage the people, places, and things in their lives. They have so over-adapted to their external environments that they have lost touch with their internal lives—not just with their needs, but with the feelings, fantasies, desires, longings, loves, dreams and ambitions that define them as unique individuals.

They also tend to be people who identify with their thoughts, not their feelings. Ask "How are you feeling?" and they'll tell you what they think.

But without access to feelings, we cannot even understand our own thought processes.

> To know what we think, we must know how we feel. It is feeling that shapes belief and forms opinion. It is feeling that directs the strategy of argument. It is our feelings, then, with which we must come to honorable terms.[10]

Joseph Campbell:

> You see, consciousness thinks it's running the shop. But it's a secondary organ of a total human being, and it must not put itself in control. It must submit and serve the humanity of the body.[11]

I'll often begin therapy with such clients by explaining the difference between inner-directed and outer-directed people.

> *Inner-directed people know how to go inside and listen for instructions. They listen to what they're feeling, sensing, and wanting, and they use what they hear when making choices. Outer-directed people are focused outside. They look for external guidance or permission or reassurance or rules to follow. Which kind of person are you?*

This usually marks the start of a conversation they've been needing to have for years, even decades.

In a way, all the above merely restates what I said earlier about needing feelings to tell us what we need. Because the single most important emotional need is to be authentic, to live as oneself. And without access to our feelings, one cannot know what that self is.

Some people argue that feelings are something you have, not something you are. This is true. We are more than our feelings, just as we are more than any other part of us, like our head or our heart.

But we cannot be ourselves without our head or our heart.

And the same goes for our feelings.

CONNECTION

We also need access to feelings in order to connect with other human beings emotionally.

Emotional connection is what happens when people come out of hiding, express themselves authentically, and feel seen, heard, and valued by each other.

This is a nonnegotiable need.

We are social animals, tribal animals. We live, reproduce, work, and flourish in groups. So strong is our need for each other that the worst punishment humans can suffer, short of death, is prolonged solitary confinement.

But we need more than just to be around other people. Proximity is not connection. Watch riders on a subway, inches apart physically, light years apart emotionally. To be among other people but emotionally disconnected is to be lonely in a crowd.

Connection is essential to sanity, even to our sense that we are human.

And yet needing something is not the same thing as knowing how to find or create it. I meet many people who are starved for connection, yet unable to feed themselves. All therapists do. It's probably the main reason we have therapists in the first place.

Some people have nowhere else to go to express themselves freely and feel seen, heard, and valued. Some have been traumatized by abuse; others were driven into hiding by their dysfunctional families. Many have been socialized into neurosis by having to adapt to a culture that penalizes emotional authenticity. But all are crippled by control addiction and trapped behind their social masks. Fritz Perls:

> If you wear a mask, you are in touch with the inside of the mask. Anyone trying to touch you with eyes or hands will merely make contact with the mask. Communication, the basis of human relationships, is impossible.[12]

This is an important point. *Control and healthy communication are antithetical.* Healthy communication requires honesty, intimacy, vulnerability, spontaneity, and above all, safety. None of these is compatible with an addiction that overcontrols our feelings and tries to manipulate our image in another person's eyes.

For many such people the treatment of choice is group therapy. Group is a place where they can experience (often for the first time) the healing that comes from connecting emotionally with others. What makes this healing possible is shared feelings.

Members usually enter with a wide variety of problems, histories, and personalities, differing in age, gender, socioeconomic status, and personal taste. What they share are four basic emotional needs (attention, acceptance, approval, and affection) and four basic emotional responses (mad, sad, glad, and scared). Each knows what these feel like, and over time this knowledge allows them to understand and accept each other. This doesn't happen automatically, of course. It requires time, testing, experimentation, and taking risks. But when it does happens, members start to feel attached to each other in much the same way members of a healthy family do. Feelings are the glue.

Only connect.

~ E. M. Forster

ALIVE

Finally, without access to our emotional radar, we cannot feel fully alive.

We can live, of course. We can survive.

But as what, exactly?

We've all known people who have died emotionally but continue to walk among us. Some lead mechanical lives, lives of routine, predictability, and sameness. Some lead lives that are entirely intellectual, reducing all feelings to thoughts and trying to think their way through every experience and problem. Some lead lives of hectic numbness, using any means possible to sedate or distract themselves from the emotional river flowing inside. And some lead constipated lives, filled with feelings that scare them but which they have never learned to understand or express or accept.

These are all forms of control addiction.

Alexander Lowen:

> We want to be more alive and feel more, but we are afraid of it. Our fear of life is seen in the way we keep busy so as not to feel, keep running so as not to face ourselves, or get high on liquor or drugs so as not to sense our being. Because we are afraid of life, we seek to control or master it.[13]

Compare this over-controlled life to a life of feelings:

> I want a life that sizzles and pops and makes me laugh out loud. And I don't want to get to the end, or to tomorrow, even, and realize that my life is a collection of meetings and pop cans and errands and receipts and dirty dishes. I want to eat cold tangerines and sing out loud in the car with the windows open and wear pink shoes and stay up all night laughing and paint my walls the exact color of the sky right now. I want to sleep hard on clean white sheets and throw parties and eat ripe tomatoes and read books so good they make me jump up and down, and I want my every day to make God belly laugh, glad that he gave life to someone who loves the gift.[14]

THE RISK OF FEELING

And yet, despite all of the above, most of us end up seeing emotional life as a problem. We treat feelings as, at best, inconvenient or embarrassing, at worst risky or dangerous. And we try to use control to put that puppy on a leash.

Lowen argues that we seek to control life because we are afraid of it. But which is the chicken and which is the egg?

Do we try to control life because we fear it, or do we fear life because it resists our need for control?

I don't know.

But I don't think it matters.

To me, fear of feelings and the wish for control are inextricably bound together. Talk about one and you end up talking about the other. So as a practical matter—that is, a therapeutic issue—I have to tackle both problems at the same time.

People come to therapy because they want to feel better. This is a legitimate goal. Nobody should spend their life suffering. I agree with the Dalai Lama:

The very purpose of our life is to seek happiness.[15]

But *happy* is not the same thing as *painless*. And there is no such thing as a painless life.

My job as a therapist, then, is to help people find happiness despite the inescapable pains of living.

To help them re-embrace feeling, despite the risk.

With control addicts, the first steps to doing that job are the three I have followed so far in this book:

- I help them see controlling as an addiction.

- I help them see how this addiction makes them sick.

- I help them see that the real goal of controlling is feelings, and why over controlling feelings does not work.

In the end, over-controlling feeling fails for two simple reasons: feelings cannot and should not be controlled.

I've explained above why feelings should not be controlled, how we need them to defend against danger, identify needs, know ourselves, connect with others, and feel fully alive.

That feelings *cannot* be controlled is perhaps less obvious.

The best way I know to explain that is by pointing to the paradoxical nature of control.

THREE PARADOXES

A paradox is "a statement that is seemingly contradictory or opposed to common sense and yet is perhaps true."[16]

Three paradoxes govern the functioning of control.

The first paradox is:

The more control you need, the less in control you feel.

The second paradox is:

The more you try to control other people, the more you force them to control you back.

The third paradox is:

To get more control in one place, you must give it up in another.

The first paradox is *intrapsychic,* operating within the controller's own mind. The second is *interpersonal,* governing interactions between people. And the third is *existential,* rooted in the nature of existence itself.

Let's discuss these in more detail.

THE MORE YOU NEED

The more control you need, the less in control you feel.

— THE FIRST PARADOX

People who say they want to feel *in control* usually mean they want to feel calm, safe, settled and secure.

But using control to achieve security is self-defeating. It's the emotional equivalent of trying to put out a fire with gasoline.

This paradox takes many forms, but two common examples should suffice. One is anxiety management. As noted earlier, we tend to be afraid of feelings. We often express this fear by holding them inside. But instead of making us feel safe, suppressing feelings actually raises our anxiety. Paul Foxman:

When feelings are denied or kept inside there is typically a buildup of physical tension. When that tension is not released, an internal pressure builds up. An accumulation of such pressure leads to anxiety, due to fears of losing control emotionally. That condition also triggers anxiety because of its physiological similarity to the fight/flight response, which is normally associated with danger. Thus our personality creates a paradox in which we deny feelings to prevent anxiety but experience anxiety when we deny our feelings.[17]

Alexander Lowen agrees:

It is not generally recognized that suppression of a feeling makes one afraid of that feeling. It becomes a skeleton in the closest one dares not look at. The longer it is hidden, the more frightening it becomes.[18]

This is the problem of emotional constipation I discussed earlier (see chapter 24). Feelings are meant to be expelled, not buried. Buried feelings don't dissipate; they collect.

Clients who fear their own anger need to be encouraged to express it in session, and those afraid of grief need to be encouraged to cry, and the chronically frightened need to be helped to identify and express their anxieties whenever they come up. Only when this happens can one begin to feel calm inside.

A second area in which the First Paradox operates is that of self-improvement.

Some clients enter therapy declaring their wish to be "better people." What they mean varies. Some want to be better spouses or parents or better at their jobs. Some want to be more disciplined, more honest, or braver. All valid goals.

But every self-improvement project that springs from self-judgment and self-rejection is doomed to fail. Fritz Perls writes,

> We are all concerned with the idea of change, and most people go about it by making programs. They want to change. "I should be like this" and so on and so on. What happens is that the idea of deliberate change never, never, never functions. As soon as you say, "I want to change"— make a program—a counter-force is created that prevents you from change. Changes are taking place by themselves. If you go deeper into what you are, if you accept what is there, then a change automatically occurs by itself."

Perls is describing what Gestaltists call the Paradoxical Theory of Change:

> *The more you try to change yourself, the more you stay stuck. But the moment you accept yourself as you are, change happens by itself.*

In therapy, my job is to help people be who they are now— their feelings and needs especially—instead of self-controlling their way into some new improved version. Until they can do this they remain internally split, into judge and defendant, controller and controlled, and all their energy gets wasted in an exhausting and futile fight against themselves.

BOOMERANG

The more you try to control other people, the more you force them to control you back.

— THE SECOND PARADOX

Most people freely admit hating to be controlled and to resisting it however they can.

But for some reason, they tend to forget that others feel the same way. They regularly try to control the people in their lives and are surprised when those people react just as they would themselves.

I see this all the time in family work.

Parents in particular seem unable to anticipate that their kids will resist being controlled by them. It's as if they believe parents *should* have control and that kids should simply acquiesce. Their narcissistic blindness in such matters sometimes takes startling forms.

A father insists his son be truthful in all things. He also judges and criticizes the boy whenever the truth he tells displeases Dad. Unable to see how his reaction actually discourages truth telling, he is genuinely surprised when Junior turns into a habitual liar. (Lying, of course, is the son's way of controlling Dad back.)

One mother regularly searches her adolescent daughter's room, cell phone, and social media postings for evidence that the girl is having sex. Then she is astounded when (you guessed it) the girl turns up pregnant. Though I doubt that the daughter got pregnant intentionally, it is hard to ignore what a powerful Fuck you, Mom *message it conveys.*

Dad brings his depressed son for counseling and stays to explain the problem. "He never expresses feelings," Dad complains. "Looks like he's expressing some now," I reply, nodding at the son, sitting sullen and silent on my sofa. "You look like you'd rather be anywhere else but here," I tell Junior. "That's not an option," Dad interrupts. "Okay," he snaps at the boy, "come on. Open up." Predictably, the therapy goes nowhere.

Note how, in these examples, each parent's *overt* controlling is countered by *covert* controlling by the child. (See chapter 7.) Yes, some kids openly defy their parents, but covert and unconscious resistance (like the pregnant daughter's) is much more common. Kids may feel emotionally outgunned by parental authority, but that doesn't mean they're helpless.

And then there are times when kids don't resist the controlling. They try to comply, but parents are still left feeling out of control.

An insecure mom intent on impressing the neighbors demands high achievement from her son and her daughter. Both kids try their best. The daughter gets straight A's and becomes captain of the cheerleading squad. The son makes Honor Society and wins the lead in his school play. Then, in her senior year, the daughter breaks under the pressure, swallows a bottle of Excedrin, and ends up in a psych ward. A year later the son gets drunk, drives Mom's car through a neighbor's yard, and is arrested. Mom can't see her role in these tragedies. "They're my whole life," she cries. "How can they do this to me?"

The Second Paradox shows up regularly in marital work, too, where controlling by spouses boomerangs more often than not.

One form familiar to all couples therapists is the *Pursuer/Distancer dynamic*, where one partner chases and the other runs away. The pursuer is always demanding more of something— more time, attention, affection, money, sex—and the other is always refusing or evading the demand. It's like a self-perpetuating dance in which each partner's move triggers the others: pursing provokes distancing and distancing provokes pursuit. Even when I point this out and the couple sees what they're doing, it can be impossible to get either partner to change.

Instead they play You Go First. *I'd stop chasing him if he'd give me what I want. I'd give her what she wants if she'd leave me alone.* And the dance continues.

For years now I've begun every marital and family therapy by spending time alone with each of the individuals involved. I do this because we're all control addicts, and this addiction causes most of our emotional problems, including those that emerge in relationships. So we need to address our individual addiction before those relationships can be healed.

We need to identify why we control and how we control and how our controlling hurts the people we love. Most of all, we need to see how our controlling hurts us.

Because in the end our relationships with others can't be any healthier than our relationship with ourselves.

The more you try to control other people, the more you force them to control you back.
~ *The Second Paradox of Control*

TRADEOFF

To get more control in one place, you must give it up in another.

— THE THIRD PARADOX

I once met a *speedcuber*, one of those people who could solve Rubik's Cube in 60 seconds. Nice friendly young guy. I hated him.

I was jealous. Life always felt to me just like one big, insoluble Rubik's Cube. I could never get things under control on all sides at once. The harder I tried to make one side of my cube all one color, the more infuriatingly multicolored the other sides got.

It's still like that. I still can't get everything right at once. I can see clients or do chores around the house. I can spend time with my family or work on my book. I can go to dinner with friends or clean the garage. I can keep up with my professional reading or read mysteries to relax. The one thing I can't do is everything. I'm trading off all day long.

I am not alone. Every day I talk with people whose determined attempt to get control over one area of their lives triggers a loss of control in another. Like:

The drinker who uses alcohol to manage his feelings, then loses control of his health.

The careerist who achieves success and status at work, but becomes estranged from his wife and kids.

The compulsive mother who makes her children the focus of her existence, then loses her husband to an affair.

The depressive who successfully hides his feelings from everyone, then one morning finds himself too exhausted to get out of bed.

And so on.

Earlier I mentioned Fritz Perls' idea that all attempts at self-change will trigger a resistance from deep within ourselves. That seems to be how change works in the larger world, too. The more we try to force reality to meet our expectations, the more reality pushes back.

It is a point made by cautionary tales as old as Midas and Scrooge, and as modern as *Jurassic Park*.

And it is especially relevant to those of us who struggle with addiction to control. We should remember that, in the world of feelings and relationships no less than the physical world, Newton's Third Law of Motion pertains:

For every action, there is an equal and opposite reaction.

The scales always get balanced somehow.

The same point is spelled out in a letter to Carl Jung from one of his longtime patients:

By keeping quiet, repressing nothing, remaining attentive, and by accepting reality—taking things as they are, and not as I wanted them to be—by doing all this, unusual knowledge has come to me, and unusual powers as well, such as I could never have imagined before. I always thought that when we accepted things, they overpowered us in some way or other. This turns out not to be true at all, and it is only by accepting them that one can assume an attitude towards them. So now I intend to play the game of life, being receptive to whatever comes to me, good and bad, sun and shadow forever alternating, and in this way, also accepting my own nature with its positive and negative sides. Thus everything becomes more alive to me. What a fool I was! How I tried to force everything to go according to the way I thought it ought to.[20]

THE ILLUSION OF CONTROL

I have been arguing that whenever we seek control, what we really want is to control our feelings. And I have argued that feelings both cannot and should not be controlled.

That second idea is much harder to accept than the first.

The wish to control feelings—to feel what only we want to feel, and not what we don't—lies at the root of the illusion of control. Despite all evidence, this illusion persists.

Judith Viorst:

> [M]ost of us behave as if we're the authors of our own fate, as if the ground is steady beneath our feet, as if we can rise every morning and enter into a life that we will be able to

shape by our needs, our choices, our actions, and our will. Most of us behave as if we do possess significant control.[21]

The illusion persists because, frankly, we need it. We may need the illusion even more than we need control itself.

This idea that we can control emotional life is a *necessary fiction*. Necessary fictions are stories we tell ourselves to help us get through life. They're not lies, exactly. Nor are they entirely the truth. They're more like aspirations—a way of reaching towards what we need or want.

They makes us feel better about ourselves or life or the future. They make pain, fear, and disappointment more bearable. Necessary fictions give us courage, give us hope, and help us cope.

We all live by such fictions. We all tell ourselves stories about who we are and what we're doing and where it will all lead:

Everything will be fine.

We'll live happily ever after.

I'll never get old and sick.

I'll never die.

The people I love will never die.

Money can buy happiness.

Driving is safe.

If I vote for X, it will make a difference.

Tomorrow's another day.

What makes these fictions necessary? Monkeymind. That incessant stream of anxious remembering and projecting, interpreting and analyzing, worrying and agonizing. Necessary fictions act as a sedative. They appease monkeymind, quiet it down.

But there's a big difference between relying on necessary fictions and being lived by them. We must remember that our fictions are fictions. To forget that is to lose touch with reality.

And that is the challenge we face when it comes to the illusion of control.

Control addicts convince themselves that control is both possible and necessary. So they spend their lives chasing it, like a commuter ten steps behind a train he can never catch. Which results in lives of frustration and misery.

My work in therapy has two goals: (a) to help people see the illusion of control as just that, an illusion, and then (b) to replace it with something that works better.

For more on the latter, read on.

PART IV

PLAN B

Problems are never solved at the same
level of thinking that created them.

— ALBERT EINSTEIN

BOTTOM

If you bring forth what is within you,
what you bring forth will save you.
If you do not bring forth what is within you,
what you do not bring forth will destroy you.

— THE GOSPEL OF THOMAS

Control addicts are just like other addicts.

And their recovery starts in the same place.

The lucky ones experience a moment when the pain of their addiction outweighs their fear of giving it up. This moment is called *hitting bottom*.

But that's not quite accurate.

Because we don't really hit bottom.

Bottom hits us.

Bottom is a realization, not a choice. It's the end result of a long process, an accumulation of emotional evidence you didn't even know you were collecting.

It's like for years you've been piling pennies on one side of a scale. Hitting bottom is that moment when the scale finally tips, your pain overwhelms your fear, and suddenly you know in your bones *I can't do this anymore.*

This happens despite all wishes and explanations to the contrary. Reality forces you to look it in the face and accept it.

It's at once an awful moment and a wonderful one. An experience of both exhaustion and relief. Because when you finally accept that you *can't* control something, you can finally stop trying to.

You can stop asking yourself *Should I let go?* and *Can I let go?* and *What will happen if I do?*

Now only one question matters: *How do I let go?*

Control is only a
temporary solution.

COOKBOOK

How to let go? has no one-size-fits-all answer.

Your answer will be as individual as your personal life, and you will evolve it just as your life evolves—gradually, through trial and error.

Recovery is not like following a recipe. It's more like writing a cookbook.

You write it by collecting and combining ingredients. The first ingredient is a series of questions you ask yourself.

How do I know I'm a control addict?

What parts of Monkeytraps *echo my experience?*

Where is this addiction hurting my life?

Who else is it hurting besides me?

The answers should give you an idea of where you want your recovery to focus. Violet Weingarten asks:

> Is life too short to be taking shit, or is life too short to mind it?[22]

Some of us will decide recovery means we need to stop taking shit. That means we'll work on coming out of hiding, speaking up, fighting back, and setting boundaries.

Others of us will decide recovery means we need to stop minding shit. That means we'll focus on practicing acceptance, detachment, patience and compassion.

Some of us will decide to work on one thing now, the other later.

And some of us will work on both.

There's no right way.

There's only your way, the one you create as you go along.

You create it by experimenting, risking, and learning from other people who are trying to recover.

SEVEN STONES

A third ingredient of recovery is a series of core ideas.

There are seven of them, which you learn and internalize over time. They are your own personal versions of some important truths.

Think of them as foundation stones for the new emotional life you're building.

You may use different words than I do to describe them. But my versions of these truths include the following statements:

- Recovery means addition, not subtraction.

- Recovery means exchanging control for power.

- Recovery means refocusing from outside to inside.

- Recovery means undoing at least some of our socialization.

- Recovery means embracing practice.

- Recovery means getting support.

- Recovery means some sort of enlightenment.

Explanations follow.

ADDITION

Some control addicts get nervous when we first talk about recovery. They naturally assume that recovery requires abstinence, means giving up all their controlling.

"I can't live without *some* control," they say.

Of course you can't. Nobody's asking you to.

Recovery from addiction isn't about sacrificing something necessary or valuable. It's about replacing something that doesn't work with something that does.

For example, it means exchanging compulsive behaviors for healthier alternatives. We reviewed some of those behaviors in Part 2: suppressing feelings, self-medicating with substances, manipulating other people, falsifying ourselves, relying mainly on unconscious defenses (like projection and transference) to manage anxiety, and blindly following the Plan A you learned as a child.

In recovery we work on gradually exchanging those behaviors for three main alternatives to control. Called *surrender, responsibility,* and *intimacy,* they are discussed in detail below.

Recovery also means replacing a dysfunctional goal with one that's more achievable. The dysfunctional goal is *actual control* over reality. The more achievable goal is *a sense of control,* that feeling also known as calm, acceptance, patience, hope, faith, serenity, and peace of mind.

More than anything else, though, recovery means replacing the idea of control with the idea of power.

Good therapy
does not
leave you
better adjusted.

It leaves you
more
yourself.

POWER

Control and power are not the same thing.

Control means being able to dictate reality, to force life itself—people, places, and things—to meet our expectations.

But *power* means being able to take care of yourself, to get your needs met without losing yourself in the process—to not just survive but to heal, grow, and be happy.

They're not just different, control and power. Sometimes they're opposites.

🔲 Power is a real possibility, where control is often an illusion.

🔲 Power is healthy, where control is often pathological.

- Power is rooted in self-acceptance and confidence, where control grows out of insecurity and fear.

- Power makes you stronger, where control weakens you, can even make you sick.

- Power attracts people to one another, where control tends to drive them apart.

But the most important difference between them is:

- Power is something only an adult can develop, where control is the basic survival skill of a child.

Think about it. If I'm a kid, I can't take care of myself. I need big people to feed me, clothe me, protect me, love me. Without big people, I die.

And because I know this at the deepest level, I learn early on to stay on their good side—to please and appease them, avoid their anger, meet their expectations. To be what big people want me to be, instead of who I am.

This is inevitable. It's also how control addicts are born.

Control addicts keep feeling and functioning like kids instead of developing personal power. They keep pleasing and appeasing and manipulating the way children do. They never come out of hiding, never learn to be themselves out loud.

Externally, they look like adults. Inside, they still feel like kids who need support, approval, or permission from big people.

Recovery is about reversing this.

Recovery is about finally growing up inside.

REFOCUSING

Refocusing attention is one key to developing power.

Our need to refocus comes from realizing the real reason we try to control stuff: We're trying to control *how we feel*.

We're especially trying to manage anxiety.

Think about it. What scares you the most? Failure? Criticism? Rejection? Abandonment? Humiliation? Loneliness? Physical pain or discomfort?

That's what you feel most compelled to control.

Compulsive means *anxiety-driven*. Whenever I act like a control addict—when, for example, I...

- Hide my real self from other people

- Hide my true feelings from myself

- Try to impress, coerce, or manipulate others

- Insist things be done my way

- Rescue or caretake friends or family members

- Worry endlessly about the future, or

- Try to make my environment just as I want it to be

...I'm being driven by anxiety over what will happen if I don't do these things.

Recovery means finding another way to manage this anxiety, This is where refocusing comes in.

When I refocus, I shift my attention from Out There to In Here. I redefine the problem from some external trigger (*X looks mad*) to my own reaction (*I'm scared of X*).

I step back from that reaction and realize that, to feel safe again, I really don't need to control X. I just need to change my reaction. If I can do that, X's anger stops being a problem.

Changing my reaction to stuff is what allows me to stop trying to control it.

MAN VS. SUIT

A man goes to a tailor and asks for a new suit. The tailor takes his measurements and tells him to come back in a week. A week later the man stands in his new suit before the tailor's mirror. "How do you like it?" the tailor asks. "Beautiful," the man says. "Except one sleeve is longer than the other." "No problem," says the tailor, "just raise your shoulder a little." The man does; the sleeves even out. "Okay," says the man, "but one pant leg is longer than the other." "No problem," says the tailor, "just raise your hip a little." The man does; the pants even out. He pays for the suit and limps out of the tailor's shop with his shoulder and hip raised. On the sidewalk he passes two women. "My goodness," one whispers, "Did you see that poor deformed man?". "Yes," replies her friend. "But such a beautiful suit."

The man in the suit is every socialized human being.

Socialization, again, is the process whereby individuals are trained to adapt to their group, to conform, to be normal.

In the process, they lose some of their individuality. Worse, that same process twists them out of shape, bends their minds and feelings and perceptions and even their bodies into forms acceptable to others but inauthentic, uncomfortable, even painfully unhealthy for the suit-wearers themselves.

"It is no sign of health to be well adjusted to a profoundly sick society," wrote Jiddu Krishnamurti.

That's why I believe recovery means undoing at least some of how we've been socialized.

Now, I'm not talking here about becoming an outlaw, an eccentric or a crazy person. I'm talking about revisiting compromises you may need to rethink.

It could be the career you chose, or people with whom you associate, or even the person you married. It could be where you live, the church you attend, the party that gets your vote each November. It could be the therapist you see weekly, or some group to which you belong. It could be any important decision you made out of fear instead of honesty, or any choice made with your attention focused outward instead of on what you were feeling inside.

I sometimes encourage clients to think about all this by asking: "What did you want to be when you grew up?" Often a wistful look comes into their eyes, which is then replaced by sadness as they notice the distance between what they once wanted and what they now have.

I don't know what suit you've contorted your way into. Probably you don't either. I do know that socialization squeezes us all into suits that don't quite fit. And I'm pretty sure that you'll begin to realize this when you try to give up controlling.

This is essential work. You need to discover how well the life you've created for yourself meets your real needs and how the people around you react to the real you.

Yes, this can be scary. It's why both practice and emotional support are so essential to recovery.

The more you are like the others, the more secure you will feel, yet the more your heart will ache, the more your dreams will be troubled, and the more your soul will slip off into silences. ~ *James Hollis*

PRACTICE

Tourist: Can you tell me how to get to Carnegie Hall?

New Yorker: Practice.

— OLD JOKE

Once I wrote a blog post about power and a reader replied, "Okay, I get it. Power means detaching from others and practicing self-care. I want to do that. But how? Can you be more specific?"

Not really. I don't know your needs or challenges or what you want to change about yourself or your life.

But if you want to become powerful, there's one thing you will need to learn: how to practice.

You're out for a walk and you come to a fork in the path. The right fork goes uphill and the left fork goes down. Why fight gravity? you ask yourself, and you take the left fork.

Further on you come to another fork and the same choice: right fork uphill, left fork down. Again you take the path of least resistance. You bear left.

You keep walking and making the same choice.

At the end of the hour you find yourself deep in a valley.

Now you have to climb out.

Most of us live in a valley we entered over decades by following the path of least resistance. If we want power, we'll have to climb out. And climbing out takes practice.

Self-care's not easy or everyone would do it. Most of us aren't taught to listen to ourselves and respect what we hear. Most of us are scared to do what's best for us regardless of the needs or opinions of others. Most of us find it easier to adapt to our immediate environment, to look around at what others expect and try to meet those expectations if we can. That's the downhill path, the path of least resistance.

But practice means going uphill at least some of the time.

It means choosing growth (which often hurts) over comfort.

It means risking the unfamiliar (which is scary) instead of clinging to what we already know.

It means making a plan and sticking to it, even when we stop wanting to.

Especially then.

It means delaying gratification, forgoing immediate results, and replacing them with patience and faith in the way we learn.

Finally, it means changing what we value.

We all value success. But real practice means valuing process, not product. Not the end result, but the doing itself. Regardless of our goal—learning meditation or piano, painting landscapes, growing orchids, or developing the courage to speak your mind—real practice means learning to lose yourself in the moment. Forgetting tomorrow and taking pleasure in right here, right now.

"The path is the goal," Mark Epstein writes.[23]

Real practice means loving practice itself.

TRIBE

A guy falls in a deep hole and can't climb out. "Help!" he shouts. A doctor stops by the edge of the hole. "Doc, can you help me out?" The doctor scribbles a prescription, tosses it into the hole and walks on. "Help!" the guy shouts again. A priest stops by the edge of the hole. "Father, can you help me out?" The priest scribbles a prayer, tosses it into the hole and leaves. "Help!" the guy shouts again. His best friend stops by the edge of the hole. "Joe, I'm stuck. Can you help me out?" The friend jumps down into the hole. "Are you crazy?" the guy shouts. "Now we're both down here!" "Yes," says his friend. "But I've been here before, and I know the way out."

There are three reasons why emotional support is indispensable to recovery.

1. *We are shaped by our relationships, for good or for ill. We didn't*

create our Plan A all by ourselves, and we won't develop Plan B alone either. We are profoundly social animals. Because we need people, and because we are all wounded in relationships, it is only in relationships that we will heal.

2. *Healthy relationship is essential to recovery from any addiction.* Addicts don't trust other people. That's why they're addicts. It's because they distrust people that they turn to substances or compulsive behaviors to manage their feelings. But recovery means building people back into your emotional life and learning to trust relationships, perhaps for the first time.

3. *Trust in relationships is necessary practice for control addicts,* since trust is itself an act of faith, of surrendering control.

For all these reasons, we need a support system. We need a healthy tribe.

For some people this need is met by self-help fellowships like Alcoholics Anonymous, Al-Anon, and CODA. The 12 Steps which structure these groups are, in fact, designed to help members overcome control addiction. (Though I find I sometimes need to translate some of their language. For example, Step One begins *Admitted we were powerless over x.* I have always translated this as *Admitted we could not control...* See chapter 59, about how control and power differ.) Other clients receive similar benefits from support groups, yoga classes, meditation sanghas, drumming circles—any group that combines authentic connection with emotional safety.

But if none of those appeals to you, it might be time to try therapy.

You may need the corrective emotional experience of a relationship with someone who knows and understands the real you. You may need some of the emotional feeding your Plan A omitted, some attention, acceptance, approval, and/or affection.

Ultimately, I think the treatment of choice for control addicts is group therapy. Being in a safe place where you can be yourself and not get punished for it can be transformational. Another gift of group is the experience of commonality. New members tend to enter group keenly sensitive to how they differ from others in the room. But if they stay, and the group is a healthy one, they end up increasingly aware of how everyone is like everyone else.

This is another essential discovery.

Because nobody recovers alone.

And a Plan B that fails to address your need for other people is just Plan A in disguise.

LIGHT BULB

The enlightened person is said to be in the world but not of it.[24]

— MARK EPSTEIN

Finally, I think any recovery worthy of the name includes a certain amount of enlightenment.

By *enlightenment* I mean an experience which changes everything.

Not out in the world, of course., Everything in your head. Which in the end amounts to the same thing.

Enlightenment means more than learning something new.

It's learning that wakes you up, opens your eyes, shifts your perceptions. It's learning that raises your understanding of yourself, other people, or life itself by a notch or two.

In other words, learning that changes you permanently.

The client who described his first Al-Anon meeting as "like a light coming on in a dark room" was having that sort of experience. So does the addict who hits bottom and all of a sudden sees the utter futility of Plan A.

The idea of enlightenment connotes two other gifts to me.

One gift is humility. "Enlightenment is permanent," writes Chogyam Trungpa, "because we have not produced it; we have merely discovered it."[25] Stumbling across a larger truth tends not to inflate ego, but to shrink it.

The other gift is freedom. Enlightenment produces a clarity of vision most people lack, which in turn reduces freedom from delusion and confusion. It shows us how things really are, how the world really works. "Suddenly I could see all the furniture I've been tripping over all my life," said my Al-Anon client. It is in this sense that the enlightened are *in* the world but not *of* it.

Most of all, I like the description of enlightenment offered by Zen master Joko Beck:

> Enlightenment is not something you achieve. It is the absence of something. All your life you have been going

forward after something, pursuing some goal. Enlightenment is dropping all that.[26]

I like this because it reminds me of something I've been hearing for years from clients who've begun to free themselves from control addiction. They all use the very same words to describe their new life:

"It's so much *easier.*"

Almost any person, no matter how damaged and poisoned and blinded, is infinitely more capable of intelligence and of joy than he can let himself be or than he usually knows.

~ *James Agee*

THREE QUESTIONS

Enough generalizing. Down to specifics.

As a practical matter, every recovery starts with three questions:

1. What am I trying to control here?

2. Have I been able to control this before?

And if the answer to the second question is No, "no":

3. What can I do instead?

These are essential questions to ask ourselves when stressed, because they remind us that (a) stress is what usually triggers our controlling and (b) our controlling usually produces more stress.

Not always easy to answer, though.

Because each is a trick question.

1. WHAT AM I TRYING TO CONTROL HERE?

Control addicts answer this by looking outside themselves, at externals. *I want my spouse to stop criticizing me. I want more money in the bank. I want my son to pass math.*

But don't be tricked. Remember that what we really want to control is feelings. Your spouse's criticism hurts you; lack of money makes you feel insecure; your son's grades are embarrassing. So what you really want is to eliminate hurt, insecurity, and embarrassment.

That's good news, since feelings tend to be easier to manage than externals.

2. HAVE I BEEN ABLE TO CONTROL THIS IN THE PAST?

Same trick here. Focus on feelings.

Say you tried to control your spouse's criticism by apologizing, appeasing, or retaliating. Did any of that leave you feeling less hurt or angry?

Say you tried to control your finances by working harder, worrying more, or nagging family members about their spending. Did any of that eliminate your insecurity?

Say you tried to control your son's grades by yelling, punishing, or standing over him while he did homework. Did any of that reduce your embarrassment? Or just create more tension and conflict?

If your honest answer to this second question is Yes, terrific. Problem solved. Keep doing what you're doing.

But if your answer is No, it's probably time for a less controlling solution.

3. WHAT CAN I DO INSTEAD?

Here the trick is to remember the three alternatives to control mentioned earlier: surrender, responsibility, and intimacy.

THREE ALTERNATIVES

Surrender is the ability to give up controlling what you can't control anyway. It grows out of realizing that you can let go of control and things will still be okay. Often described with words like *detachment*, *acceptance* and *faith*, surrender is the spiritual alternative to control.

Responsibility is the ability to reply to a situation honestly and with self-awareness. It grows out of listening to your feelings (instead of hiding or editing them) and trusting that what they tell you is both friendly (not to be feared) and important (not to be ignored). Often described with words like *presence*, *mindfulness* and *authenticity*, responsibility is the emotional alternative to control.

Intimacy is the ability to be yourself with another person and allow them to do the same with you. It's actually a combination of the first two alternatives, since it requires that you both (a) abstain from controlling someone (surrender) and (b) share the truth about yourself (responsibility). Intimacy is the interpersonal alternative to control, and represents the high-water mark of emotional development—i.e., it's about as healthy as we human beings get.

By the way, I didn't invent these alternatives. I just noticed and named them.

They're what all addicts who no longer want to be ruled by addiction—to control or to anything else—must practice in recovery.

Let's see how they look in actual practice.

SURRENDER

Surrender means being able to stop controlling reality and still believe things will be okay.

What does this mean to a recovering addict?

"Surrender is the moment of accepting reality on the unconscious level," writes Stephanie Brown.

> The individual knows the deepest truth, regardless of wishes or explanations to the contrary. Defenses used in the service of denying that reality (denial and rationalization, defiance and grandiosity) no longer work...[W]hen true unconscious surrender has occurred, the acceptance of reality means that the individual can work in it and with it.[27]

To surrender means to be able, when facing some reality we cannot dictate, to accept it with courage, patience and grace.

Some people dislike the word *surrender*. To them it connotes defeat, weakness, or failure.

Fine. Call it something else. Call it *detachment*, as Al-Anon does. Or *acceptance*. Or *trust*. Or *faith*. (Chapters on these words follow.)

Call it what you like, but notice two things about surrender:

1. SURRENDER MEANS GIVING UP CONTROL WITHOUT LOSING POWER.

Remember the difference between the two? Control tries to dictate reality. Power seeks to meet needs, to take care of the self.

Now think of swimming in a swift-flowing river. Control challenges the tide, tries to overcome it. Power goes with the flow.

The river is reality. To surrender to what would otherwise overwhelm us is not failure, not weakness, just simple intelligence. And intelligence is clearly more powerful than its opposite.

2. SURRENDER IS ESSENTIAL TO SANITY.

Also notice how important surrender is to not losing your marbles.

Think about it. Imagine someone unable to ever surrender control. How could they drive on a freeway? Fly in an airplane? Eat in a restaurant? Let their kids ride a school bus? Permit a dentist to drill their tooth? Or a surgeon to remove their tonsils? Trust a therapist with their secrets? Stay sane during a hurricane?

We surrender control daily, even hourly. We have to. Without surrender, life would be a white-knuckled nightmare and peace of mind would be impossible.

NUMB

So surrender's necessary. Why, then, do we resist it?

Because reality hurts.

It was Carl Jung who defined neurosis as "the avoidance of legitimate suffering." That's also a pretty good explanation of addiction. And as noted earlier, every addiction is an addiction to control. We seek control as a way to avoid the pain of life.

We especially want to domesticate our anxiety. Buddhist therapist Mark Epstein suggests we are all driven by a wish to return to some fixed, predictable "pre-anxious state."[28] That sounds about right to me. As mentioned earlier, I call that state the Garden of Numb. It is the place every addict unconsciously seeks, one of perfect safety and no stress, where all pain and anxieties vanish, a place where they can stop feeling anything at all.

We needn't be alcoholics or heroin addicts to want to numb out. On some level we seem to see painlessness as a sort of entitlement. Ralph Keyes writes:

> The ability to muffle anxiety feels like a perk of adulthood. We cut a Faustian deal: in return for not being so anxious all the time, we agree to tune down our whole nervous system. As a result our powers of observation decline along with our sense of smell, taste and hearing.[29]

We "tune down our nervous system" by leaving the here-and-now, turning away from physical and emotional experience, and sliding instead into preoccupation with the endless chatter of monkeymind. We avoid risk, excitement, challenge, expressiveness, creativity, and all experiences that take us out of our comfort zones. We hide in routine, evade conflict, postpone conversations, skip the party, eat the same meals over and over, watch reruns on TV, let somebody else answer the door. We resign ourselves to stale familiarity.

So perhaps the first step in learning to surrender—to accepting life on life's terms, as they say in Alcoholics Anonymous—should be awareness of this unconscious wish to avoid all pain, and a conscious willingness to be more realistic in our approach to this rich and complicated business called living.

Since living in Numb isn't really living at all.

The ability to muffle anxiety feels like a perk of adulthood. We cut a Faustian deal: in return for not being so anxious all the time, we agree to tune down our whole nervous system.

~ *Ralph Keyes*

TOLERANCE

In Oliver Stone's Platoon *(1986), a soldier wounded in a firefight lies screaming while the battle rages around him. He continues to scream until his sergeant clamps a hand over his mouth. "Take. The. Pain," the sergeant hisses. The soldier subsides into whimpers.*

I watched *Platoon* twice and had two very different reactions to that scene. The first time I saw the sergeant as an insensitive brute. The second time, three decades later and after years of studying control, I saw him as a teacher delivering a vital lesson.

The lesson was: pain and suffering are not the same thing.

Pain comes when we have been injured in some way. Suffering comes when we fight the pain, refuse to tolerate it.

Pain is mandatory, suffering is optional.

Alan Watts writes:

> The human organism has the most wonderful powers of adaptation to both physical and psychological pain. But these can only come into full play when the pain is not being constantly stimulated by this inner effort to get away from it, to separate the "I" from the feeling. The effort creates a tension in which the pain thrives. But when the tension ceases, mind and body begin to absorb the pain as water reacts to a blow or cut.[30]

A tension in which pain thrives is what we call suffering.

Tolerance serves as an antidote to this tension. It can be defined as the ability to let pain be just pain and not convert it into suffering.

Tolerance means yielding instead of fighting back. Nature is full of examples of how effective a response yielding can be. Water, soft and pliable, overcomes any obstacle. The springy birch survives hurricanes that split a rigid oak. Possums survive predator attacks by playing dead, and a salamander grabbed by its tail will leave the tail in your hand and run away.

Yielding to physical and emotional pains operates similarly.

Anne Lamott tells of begging a nurse for relief from the awful sore throat that followed her tonsillectomy. The nurse denied her pain medication and suggested she chew gum instead.

She explained that when we have a wound in our body, the nearby muscles cramp around it to protect it from any more violation and from infection, and that I would need to use these muscles if I wanted to relax them again... The first bites caused a ripping sensation in the back of my throat, but within minutes all the pain was gone, permanently.

I think that something similar happens with our psychic muscles. They cramp around our wounds...to keep us from getting hurt in the same place again...So these wounds never have a chance to heal.[31]

Think of the worst wounds in your past: losses, failures, disappointments, humiliations. Notice how you have cramped around them. Now consider tolerance as an alternative.

Tolerance means not running away from pain, not denying or hiding it. It doesn't mean gritting your teeth and being brave. It means accepting pain without protest or resentment, finding some way to go with the emotional flow. As a practical matter this may mean talking about your pain for the first time, or thinking about it in a new way, or expressing feelings you may have hitherto blocked.

I think of tolerance as an emotional shock absorber, a special sort of patience with discomfort. It allows us to take a punch without collapsing, numbing out, or relapsing into compulsive control.

We recovering addicts need this shock absorber in order to

practice surrender. That's because surrender itself triggers all sorts of discomfort, especially when our practice is new. If I'm used to hiding feelings, the first time I express them will feel scary. I must learn to tolerate that scariness. If I am unused to taking care of myself, of putting my needs ahead of others, the first time I do that I will feel guilty. I'll need tolerance to get past the guilt.

But the best reason to learn tolerance is to get past pain as fast as possible.

I find that when I am able to tolerate pain, a strange thing happens. The pain stops being a problem. It still hurts, but in a different way. When I stop fighting it—stop taking the pain personally—I stop being afraid or angry. I lose the urge to run away. Pain no longer feels unfair, like a punishment I don't deserve. It becomes just a fact of life, like a bad weather day. It just is. And then I can relax and wait for it to pass.

With feelings, as a rule, the only way out is through.

DETACHMENT

Detachment is another form of surrender.

To *detach* means to step back, to disengage emotionally, to refuse to dance with an experience—to say to someone or something that invites us to control it, "Thanks, but go on without me. I'll sit this one out."

It's a word I first heard in Al-Anon, whose members used it to describe their best defense against the siren song of alcoholic pathology.

These were people who had spent years—and often, been driven nearly crazy—trying to heal, fix, rescue, persuade, coerce, punish, or manipulate their alcoholic family member into recovery. It never worked, of course, but they saw no alternative, because they were addicts themselves. They were addicted to their addicts. The boundary between them and the alcoholic was so impossibly blurred they could not distinguish their own personality or feelings or needs.

Many were children of alcoholic, abusive, or otherwise dysfunctional families which taught them control addiction as a way of life. They—we—were half grownups. On the outside we looked like adults. Inside we felt like kids, still scared and powerless, with no choice but to navigate around other people as if they were huge icebergs and we were tiny, thin-hulled ships. We hid our feelings, avoided conflict, people-pleased, and worried endlessly about what people thought of us. Over and over we lost ourselves, always in desperate hope that concealing who we were could win us some of the safety and acceptance our families could never provide.

Earlier I described codependency as a way of handling all experiences, all feelings and relationships. It's actually much more than that. It is a sort of trance one enters and then cannot escape. Learn it early enough, rely on it long enough, and it becomes a fixed and internalized belief system, a basic assumption, an unconscious way of perceiving oneself, other people, all experiences, life itself.

For codependents, the idea of detachment comes as a revelation. The revelation is that one can stop controlling externals and still survive.

As a practical matter, detachment means redrawing the psychological boundary between Me and Not Me. That boundary is like an imaginary circle you draw around yourself, a dotted line delineating where you end and the rest of the world begins. Codependents draw the line too far out, creating a circle that contains way too much.

I'm reminded of how important detachment is whenever I meet someone incapable of it.

Like Anita, who got arrested when she could not stop stalking the boyfriend she thought was cheating on her. Or Barbara, whose rage at her husband's affair finally drove her to swallow a large bottle of Excedrin (I'll show him). Or Carl, who after the 9/11 bombings stopped going to work and stayed glued to his TV screen, because watching CNN made him feel he knew what was happening and so could protect himself and his family.

Each chased the same illusion: the illusion of control. Each needed therapy to teach them to redraw their boundaries, to detach from the uncontrollable and so save themselves.

We all need this ability. For every human being with a monkeymind, detachment is a declaration of sanity, independence, and self-love.

For the recovering control addict, it is an indispensable tool. Being in recovery *means* learning detachment. What starts as a conscious decision—a waking-up from the trance—develops into a practice. Then the practice evolves into a healthy way of life.

No detachment, no recovery.

ACCEPTANCE

If the key to detachment is to step away from toxic involvement, the key to acceptance is a step into embracing who you are.

When you think about it, the reason is obvious: you can't give away what you don't have.

I can't accept others (and I mean real acceptance, not the phony codependent kind) any better than I accept myself. Can't like, love, or forgive them any better than I like, love, or forgive myself. Can't accept their feelings or limitations or mistakes or sins while inside I punish myself for my own.

Psychologist Tara Brach lists six common signs of our inability to accept ourselves:

We embark on one self-improvement project after another. We hold back and play it safe rather than risking failure. We withdraw from our experience of the present moment. We keep busy. We become our own worst critics. We focus on other people's faults.[32]

I don't know anyone who doesn't do most of these.

We don't set out consciously to judge or reject others. But self-judgment keeps us tense, scared, and in emotional pain. And there's no way to stop that tension, fear, and pain from coloring our perceptions and our encounters with other people. To pretend otherwise is at best self-ignorance, at worst denial.

You know what I'm talking about. Have you noticed how, on days when you really like yourself, everyone else seems more loveable?

Or how the world looks when self-approval feels impossible? For me, self-rejection quickly morphs into a generalized feeling of impatience and discontentment. I stiffen emotionally against everything. Bad weather seems worse, slow traffic seems slower, the rude waitress is infuriating, the bad news on TV becomes intolerable.

As with most (maybe all) emotional problems, at the heart of self-judgment lies the search for control. For some reason we think beating ourselves up will somehow make us stronger or smarter.

Fritz Perls describes what we do as "the beloved game of the neurotic, the self-torture game," where our internal *top dog* endlessly abuses our internal (and eternally guilty) *underdog*:

> So the top dog and underdog strive for control. Like every parent and child, they strive with each other for control. The person is fragmented into controller and controlled... The other day I had a talk with a friend of mine and I told her, "Please get this into your nut: mistakes are not sins," and she wasn't half as relieved as I thought she would be. Then I realized, if mistakes are not a sin any more, how can she castigate others who make mistakes?[33]

Note again the blurred boundary of the control addict, the unconscious reliance on control to evaluate both self and other, and the failure to distinguish the two. If I'm angry at me, I must be angry at you. If I'm unhappy with myself, I'll be unhappy with everything.

Working on acceptance means escaping all that.

As a practical matter, it begins with noticing what we *can't* accept, what we regularly judge or reject in ourselves. This can be painful.

I asked one chronically angry client to carry a notepad and write down each and every self-judgment she heard for a week. She came to her next session crying. "God, I'm *awful*," she whispered. But before I could reassure her, she clarified. "I mean I'm *awful to myself.*"

After that session something changed in her. Seeing her self-abuse (learned, unsurprisingly, from emotionally abusive parents) shocked her. The shock pushed her to stop. She began to soften her judgments of herself and to ask my help when she couldn't. Over time her ability to self-accept grew and as that happened, the anger she'd carried inside her since childhood diminished. Making peace with herself became a path to peace with everyone else.

Much of spiritual life is self-acceptance, maybe all of it.

~ Jack Kornfield

TRUST

In recent years, I've worked increasingly with women, especially traumatized women in therapy groups.

Some of these women suffered physical, emotional or sexual abuse in childhood. Others were traumatized as adults by abusive or otherwise toxic romantic or sexual relationships. Some had experienced both.

All entered therapy reporting "trust issues."

And virtually all misunderstood the remedy for chronic mistrust.

Some had chosen defensive withdrawal from relationships.

One rape survivor lived alone, worked from home, ignored tele-phone calls, and communicated with other people only by email. "I don't trust anyone," she told me. "I don't trust you. I wouldn't be here if my doctor hadn't told me I'd end up in a psych hospital if I didn't come."

Others chose hypervigilance. If they risked new relationships, they did so like skittish ponies—on constant alert, forever scrutinizing, analyzing, suspecting, and inevitably finding new reasons to distrust. Then they'd end the relationship and start all over again.

Still others decided that trust was simply an impossibility for them. This was especially true of adults whose trust had been betrayed by parents.

A woman molested by her father, grandfather and uncle asked me, "If you can't trust your family, why would you even want to trust anybody else?"

The majority, though, had concluded that the best remedy for trust issues was to find a completely trustworthy mate.

Of course this approach led to disappointment after disap-pointment. No mate is perfect. Everyone lies, denies, evades, and avoids responsibility sometimes. We're all insensitive, self-ignorant, stubborn, and immature. We all make mistakes. We all hurt and disappoint the people we love, often without meaning to, often without realizing it. Sometimes we're just plain dense.

So these women who hoped a white knight would heal their trust issues almost always ended up as disillusioned damsels still in distress.

Therapy with distrustful clients can be challenging. As a new therapist, my first impulse was to win them over and earn their trust. This usually backfired. *Trying* is a form of controlling, and distrustful people are exquisitely sensitive to being controlled.

So I developed another approach. The first step was to tell wary clients:

Don't trust me. Test me. See if I'm reliable. See if I lie. See if I change my tune from week to week. See if what I say rings true. Don't take my word for anything. Test me, and trust your gut. Do this for as long as you need to.

Then I did my best to relax and be myself and let their radar decide if I was trustworthy.

This usually relaxed them a little. They were going to test me, anyway, but it was nice to get permission.

The second step was to explain my view of trust. "Trust is an inside job," I'd say.

It starts not with vulnerability or a leap of faith but with self-trust.

I remember old newspaper advertisements that showed a 98-pound weakling getting sand kicked in his face by a bully at the beach. The ads were for exercise equipment. Buy the equipment, build up your muscles, then you can go kick sand in the bully's face.

That's what I mean by self-trust. Not getting strong enough to harass other people; getting strong enough to know that in any given situation, you can take care of yourself.

Can you imagine how that feels, knowing you can always take care of yourself? When you know you can do that, trust stops being a problem.

The third step was to help them develop their coping and relationship muscles. Usually this occupied the rest of the therapy, includes most of what I've said in this book so far, and most of what I'll say later about responsibility and intimacy.

Rebuilding trust is often a lifetime project. But there is no more important issue, since trust underpins everything else. Life without trust is a house built on sand. Trust in oneself and other people is essential to love, friendship, freedom, happiness, peace of mind. Trust in life itself is functionally essential to living as a sane person. And people without trust cannot help but be consumed by their addiction to control.

FAITH

Finally, we come to the idea of faith.

Faith is the antithesis to control. It is the ability to let go and believe things will work out just fine. Control addiction believes *nothing* works out just fine unless we force it to.

Earlier I called *surrender* the spiritual alternative to control. By "spiritual" I mean that part of us that acknowledges something bigger than us, bigger than mind, ego or willpower.

Faith lies at the heart of surrender. But like recovery itself, faith is highly individual. No one hands you faith off a rack. You fashion it yourself over time, out of your personal beliefs and experiences. It's the highly personal answer each individual evolves to the question: *Surrender to what?*

Five things to remember about faith:

1. ALL ADDICTS LACK FAITH

That's why they're addicts. Lack of faith leaves you no choice but to control everything, or at least how everything makes you feel.

It's also why all Twelve Step programs are essentially attempts to replace control addiction with faith in a bigger something. Often that something is something other than God. One client who belonged to Alcoholics Anonymous told me he could never believe in anything until he began to translate the word *God* as short for Group Of Drunks. "A.A. meetings saved my life," he said. "So those meetings became the one thing I could believe in."

The inability to find something bigger in which to believe turns control addiction into a life sentence. How can you ever surrender without an answer to the question *surrender to what?*

2. FAITH IS NOT RELIGION

I long ago stopped being surprised at the lack of faith in clients who describe themselves as "religious." Usually what they mean is that they identify with a particular sect or church, were raised as something in particular, attend services regularly, read religious books, or sing in the choir. They're not hypocrites, exactly. They sincerely see themselves as people of faith. But whatever they believe has not put much of a dent in their codependency. They rarely *turn it over* or *let go and let God*. When stress hits they turn, not to God, but to control.

> *One angry churchgoing couple came to weekly sessions and argued about everything under the sun, including how they felt about their pastor and other church members. Each believed firmly that they believed in God. But, as a practical matter, what they really believed in was controlling people, places, and things.*

3. FAITH IS A CHOICE

Some clients think of faith as something from outside, something they must wait for the way kids wait for Christmas. I tell them they can go out to meet it. William James wrote:

> We can act *as if* there were a God; feel *as if* we were free; consider Nature *as if* she were full of special designs; lay plans *as if* we were to be immortal; and we find then that these words do make a genuine difference in our moral life.[34]

Think of this as the "fake it 'til you make it" approach to spirituality. Want to believe in something bigger? Act as if you already do. Take the risk you'd take if you had faith and watch the results.

"Act as if ye had faith, and faith will be given to you."[35] It's an experimental approach, and I think it works just fine.

4. FAITH IS BEHAVIOR

Susan Salzberg notes that in Pali, the language of the original Buddhist texts:

> Faith is a verb, an action, as it is also in Latin and Hebrew. Faith is not a singular state that we either have or don't have, but is something that we do. We "faithe."[36]

To *faithe* can mean the act-as-if approach described above. It also means practice.

> *One man, an intellectual, attended therapy with me for years. He read books I recommended, made notes and brought them to session, and took obvious pleasure in discussing control addiction and its alternatives. I thought the therapy was going wonderfully until his wife attended a session. Then it became clear that nothing we'd talked about had filtered into his marriage. He interrupted his wife, discounted her feelings, refused to acknowledge his own, and got angry when confronted on these behaviors.*

"Faith apart from works is dead," says the Bible.[37] It's the same with therapy. Recovery without practice is just words.

5. FAITH IS EVIDENCE-BASED

Faith is often described in ways which make it sound like a leap into the unknown. And certainly the term *leap of faith* means something. Faith usually requires some sort of leap, some risk. It requires action in the absence of guarantees.

But there's always some evidence on which we base our leaps. Otherwise we wouldn't make them.

The first-time skydiver steps out the door of the plane only if he has faith in his instructor and what he has taught him. When we marry someone, we do so because experience has convinced us this is someone with whom we can share our lives. The client entering therapy for the first time does so because something she's read or been told has persuaded her that therapy *could* be helpful. Anxious clients who risk joining my therapy groups do so because they have come to know me and to trust that I'm right when I say this new experience will help and not hurt them.

But the most reliable evidence comes from faith in oneself—in your own feelings and instincts, in your ability to follow the instructions they send, and in every experience which ever reassured you that your internal radar functions adequately.

PRACTICING SURRENDER

Notes on practicing surrender:

1. Surrender is a skill you can learn and practice.

2. Surrender is a skill you *must* learn and practice.

3. The urge to control is like gravity; it pulls on us constantly. It pulls hardest when we're stressed, scared, unfocused or tired. It is at such times that practice becomes hardest and most crucial. Hey, you'll never be weightless. That's okay. With practice you can learn to fight gravity longer and longer.

4. You decide when to practice surrender by asking yourself questions listed in chapter 65: *What am I trying to control?*

Have I had any luck controlling this in the past? If not, what can I do instead?

5. Practicing surrender doesn't always mean trying something totally new. More often it means putting surrender to new use—applying it in new situations, extending it to new parts of our emotional life. You step back from something you usually try to control. That's practice. You share a feeling or preference that you usually hide. That's practice. You do it again and again until it stops feeling weird and starts feeling natural. That's how practice works.

6. Baby steps count. You practice detachment by picking what feels like the smallest tolerable risk. It could be making a scary phone call, or answering one. It could be making eye contact with eyes you'd rather avoid. Stop telling yourself *This is silly, this doesn't matter.* If it feels risky, it matters. That's how recovery progresses: step by baby step. Eventually baby steps take you to a place where you wonder why you ever did things any other way.

7. Reminders and mantras help. Reinforce your practice with the reminders Twelve Step programs use: *One day at a time, Let go and let God, Turn it over, Go with the flow.* Or create your own, based on your reading and experience. My own favorite is scribbled on a sticky note taped to my computer monitor:

    95% of what we worry about never happens.

Then there's everyone's favorite, Reinhold Niebuhr's famous Serenity Prayer.

God grant me the serenity
To accept the things I cannot change,
Courage to change the things I can,
And the wisdom to know the difference.

8. Forgive yourself for relapses. Relapse is inevitable. And understood correctly, it usually contains a kind of gift. It tells us what's missing from our recovery. Maybe you're forgetting to take care of yourself. (See chapter 59, "Power.") Maybe you're not getting enough emotional support. (See chapter 63, "Tribe.") In any case, never make relapse worse by beating yourself up over it. Think *lesson*, not *failure*. Or think of relapse as the bottom of the hill where you roll at difficult times. The more you practice, the longer you'll remain uphill.

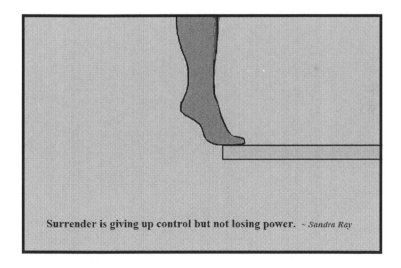

Surrender is giving up control but not losing power. ~ *Sandra Ray*

RESPONSIBILITY

I probably use the word *responsible* differently than you.

To me it means *able to respond* as in *reply* or *answer.*

Responsible people are those who can answer a situation, challenge, or problem in a healthy way—one that meets their needs, respects their feelings, acknowledges their preferences, promotes their growth, and leaves them more powerful.

I'm guessing you think *responsibility* means something else...

That may be because I've known so many clients who confuse it with following rules, meeting expectations, and discharging obligations. These "responsible" people were trained to lose themselves. They were taught to sacrifice their needs, feelings, preferences, and personal integrity to other people, jobs, imposed codes of behavior, impossible standards, or endless To Do lists. Eventually they came to do this without thinking, less out of love or discipline than self-defense. They became scared of what would happen if they *didn't* do it.

That's what I call *irresponsible*.

HEALTHY SELFISHNESS

Selfishness has an awful reputation.

My dictionary defines *selfish* as "too much concerned with one's own welfare or interests and having little or no concern for others."[38] My thesaurus lists a string of equally unlovely synonyms: *self-seeking, self-pleasing, self-advancing, self-indulgent, self-besot, self-centered, self-occupied, self-absorbed, and wrapped up in oneself...*[39]

Twenty years of doing therapy has taught me two interesting things about selfishness:

1. Most people are scared of being called selfish. They act like it's the worst thing you can say, ever, about anyone.

2. Most people with a horror of selfishness were taught to be unselfish by people who were selfish themselves.

Recall the description of narcissistic families in chapter 14. These are families where kids learn to defer their feelings and needs for the sake of parents or other family members. The message such kids grow up hearing, directly and indirectly, over and over, is:

Don't take care of your self. Take care of my self instead.

It's a poison pill, this message, because once internalized it splits you right down the middle. Half of you can't stop having a self with feelings, needs, wishes, urges, and preferences. And the other half can't stop sitting in judgment on the first.

It's this split that gives rise to anxiety, depression, addictions, compulsive controlling, the neurotic self-torture game, and a reaction to the word *selfish* that amounts to a phobia.

"Actually," I tell such clients, "you're not nearly selfish enough."

Selfishness comes in two flavors, healthy and unhealthy. *Unhealthy* selfishness is the sort my dictionary and thesaurus describe. But *healthy* selfishness is essential to emotional health and adult functioning.

Healthy selfishness amounts, in the end, to self-acceptance and self-respect. Child psychologist Dorothy Corkille Briggs suggests that strong self-respect depends on two internalized convictions:

I am loveable

("I matter and have value because I exist")

and

I am worthwhile

("I can handle myself and my environment with compe-
tence. I know I have something to offer others").[40]

These convictions form the foundation of what I call "healthy
selfishness." They are not frills; they are necessities. People
who lack them move through life psychologically wounded.

What has all this to do with responsibility?

Responsibility means reclaiming the right to value oneself,
even without permission. It means growing up emotionally,
reclaiming your body and emotions. It means learning to
self-parent. It means creating a life that fits you, instead of
twisting yourself into some ill-fitting suit. It means treating
yourself with the same respect and consideration you were
taught to show others.

Learning responsibility is your antidote to the poison pill.

LISTENING

Responsibility starts with listening.

I mean listening to yourself.

No small matter, this. It can be hard. You've spent your life listening carefully to others and ignoring the voice inside.

You had no choice in this. And it started early, even earlier than you remember.

Like when you cried and Mom looked annoyed.

Or when you wet the bed and Dad yelled.

Or grabbed a cookie and heard No, it's almost dinnertime.

Or screamed in frustration or joy and heard Keep it down.

Or were made to kiss Aunt Margaret, who had whiskers and smelled like mothballs.

Or had to eat scallops despite the fact they always made you throw up.

Or wanted to sleep more and heard Wake up, time for school.

"All children are foreigners," wrote Ralph Waldo Emerson.

By themselves these bits of socialization seem harmless enough. Basic training, right? I list them merely to point out how normal it is to be taught to listen to Mommy and disregard the voice of the self.

But *normal* is not *healthy*. And the sundering of self that seems so innocuous and necessary in childhood can become a real problem for adults, especially when never balanced by enough parental love and acceptance to make the tradeoff worthwhile.

Then follows adulthood, with its increasing external demands, chores, worries, and unrelenting busyness.

Again, normal. Again, unhealthy.

Wayne Muller writes,

> [T]he Chinese word for "busy" is composed of two characters: "heart" and "failure." When we make ourselves so

busy that we are always rushing around trying to get this or that "done," or "over with," we kill something vital in ourselves, and we smother the quiet wisdom of our heart.[41]

In short, nobody escapes childhood whole and every adult needs to recover. Some lost something.

And the process of recovery begins with a conscious, brave decision:

From here on, I will listen to myself.

When in

doubt,

listen

for instructions.

RECLAIMING THE BODY

The next step in becoming responsible is reconnecting with our body.

This, too, may be harder than it sounds.

Most people I know live estranged from their bodies, which they treat like machines whose main purpose is to ferry their heads from place to place.

This estrangement starts early. Go back to the last chapter and notice how many of those childhood instructions were orders to ignore what your body was trying to say.

It's almost dinnertime *meant "Ignore your hunger."*

Time for school meant "Ignore your need for sleep."

Keep it down *meant "Keep those feelings inside."*

Kiss Aunt Margaret *meant "Pretend to feel something you don't"* (*and probably also "Pretend you don't feel something you do"*).

Many of us still follow those same orders to this day.

When clients come into session exhausted, worried, or anxious, they usually don't have to tell me. I can see it in how they move and hold themselves. My usual approach at such times is to ask them to stop talking and do a body scan.

> *Close your eyes. Take a breath. Now check out what's happening inside. Notice where you feel tense and where you feel relaxed. Notice what feels heavy and what feels light. Notice what's warm and what's cold. What feels full and what feels empty. Where you feel strong and where you feel weak.*

I give them a few minutes for this, then ask what they found.

If they tell me their legs are tired, I move my hassock closer and ask them to put their feet up. If their neck is stiff, I put a throw pillow behind their head. If they're chilly, I give them an afghan. If their stomach feels empty, I offer a cup of water. And so on. After each adjustment I check for changes in how they feel.

Ten minutes later they usually report, with surprise, that most of their exhaustion, worry, or anxiety has gone.

This impresses most people. But it's a sort of therapeutic parlor trick, this intervention. It serves only to remind people that they have bodies, and that how those bodies feel impacts their moods. It doesn't really change things. To truly reclaim their bodies, these clients need to make it a priority and work on their own.

(If you want to do that, some suggestions follow this chapter.)

The best book I know on the connection between body and mood is *Depression and the Body* by Alexander Lowen, founder of the therapy called Bioenergetics. Lowen writes:

> There is no mental disturbance that is not also a physical disturbance. The depressed person is physically depressed, as well as mentally depressed: the two are really one, each is a different aspect of the personality. The same thing is true of every other form of so-called mental illness. The belief that it is "all in the head" is the great illusion of our time, ignoring the fundamental reality that life in all its various manifestations is a physical phenomenon.[42]

FLOOR WORK

Want to practice listening to your body?

Try this:

Find a private room with an open floor to lie on. No thick carpet, please. Bare wood or thin carpet is about right.

Lie down. No pillow, no blanket.

You'll be uncomfortable, which is the point.

Lie there with eyes closed and wait for the conversation to start.

It will begin in about 30 seconds, when your body starts making suggestions.

My ankle hurts, *it murmurs. So you rotate that joint.*

My back's sore, *it grunts. So you roll onto your side.*

My shoulder's cramped. *So you roll back to your back.*

My neck hurts. *So you curl up and pillow your head on your hands.*

Keep doing this for as long as it seems interesting or useful.

The goal is not comfort (which you'll never achieve) or endurance (no extra points for staying all night). The goal is the conversation itself.

When it works, this exercise leaves you more attentive to signals from your body and more willing to make adjustments as necessary.

WITHDRAWAL

Fritz Perls once suggested that the best way to cope with discomfort was to withdraw.

> If you do this with any uncomfortable situation, you can really pinpoint what's missing in this here-and-now situation. Very often the *there* situation gives you a cue for what's missing in the *now*...Even if you get in touch with your fantasy of being on an island or in a warm bathtub, or to any unfinished situation, this will give you a lot of support when you return to reality.[43]

I do this regularly myself. I also help clients do it in session, especially when they're having trouble identifying what they need.

It's something you can practice on your own.

First take a few deep breaths. Now do a body scan. Notice what you feel and where you feel it. Notice especially where you feel tense, uncomfortable, or stressed. Take a few minutes for this.

Now imagine where you'd go right now if you could go anywhere.

You don't need to work at creating an image. Just let one come into your mind. Whatever image comes will be the right one.

Now examine this place in detail. Imagine turning your head so you can see all around. See everything there is to see. Are you inside or outside? Alone or with people? What time of day is it? What's the weather like? Notice the light, the temperature, any sounds, any smells.

Now notice how your body feels in this place. Are you sitting, standing, or lying down? Comfortable or uncomfortable? If there's any discomfort, imagine whatever you need to make it go away.

When you're ready, come back to the present. Rescan your body one more time. Note any reductions in tension, discomfort, or stress.

When it works, this exercise (a) provides relief from the stress of the moment, (b) reconnects you with your body, and (c) helps you identify what you're currently needing or missing in the here-and-now.

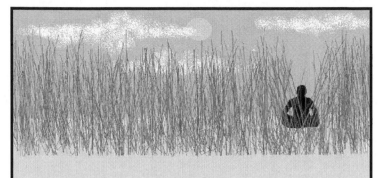

The great omission in American life is solitude -- that zone of time and space, free from the outside pressures, that is the incubator of the spirit. ~ *Marya Mannes*

NAMING FEELINGS

I wish I had a nickel for each time I asked someone *What are you feeling?* and they misunderstood the question.

I feel that you're wrong about me.

I feel my wife is a bitch.

I feel I don't know why I do what I do.

"No," I say, "those are thoughts. Feelings are *mad, sad, glad, scared*. Those are the four basic food groups. Which comes closest to what you're feeling inside?"

Here they usually hesitate. Then they ask: "What were those again?"

"Mad, sad, glad, scared. Or a variation on one of them."

Now some can then attach a label to what they're feeling.

I feel hurt and misjudged.

I'm really pissed at my wife.

It's scary to not understand myself.

Others still can't. Often they've been living in their heads for so long that the language of feelings has become foreign to them.

I ask these people to focus on their bodies.

"The body is where feelings live," I explain. "So drop down out of your head for a moment. Notice whatever's happening below the neck. Don't bother to label it, just notice. What's the first thing to come into your awareness?"

This they can usually answer.

I have a knot in my stomach.

My chest feels tight.

My heart aches.

After a few more questions *(Is this a familiar feeling? When have you felt it before?*), we're usually able to tie their physical symptoms to an underlying emotional experience.

Often just labeling their feeling (*mad, sad, glad, scared*) produces relief. The knots untie themselves, the tightness loosens, the heartache remits. Sometimes they cry.

Why am I telling you all this?

Because naming feelings is important.

It's important to be able to ask and answer the question: *What am I feeling?*

It's important to (a) knowing who you are and (b) knowing what you need.

But because we live in a world not terribly interested in our feelings, it takes practice to stay in touch with them.

So let this be an invitation or a reminder, whichever you need: go sit somewhere quiet and practice.

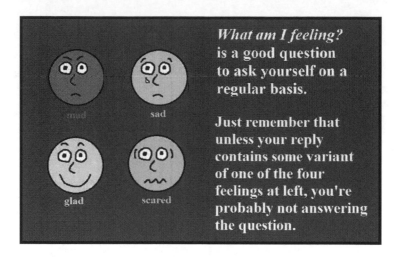

What am I feeling? is a good question to ask yourself on a regular basis.

Just remember that unless your reply contains some variant of one of the four feelings at left, you're probably not answering the question.

CHAT

This is another exercise I do on a regular basis, usually in the morning, in the car on my way to work.

It's only 10 minutes to my office, so I've learned to keep this brief and succinct.

It's a conversation with myself.

Yes, I speak both parts out loud. It felt odd at first, but now I like it. It feels real, like I'm talking to another person. Expressing feelings out loud helps to both clarify and release them in a way just *thinking* about them can't. And some mornings hearing my own voice helps me feel less isolated or lonely, like keeping myself company.

The talk is mostly about self-parenting. I check in with myself to see what I'm feeling and what I need. It usually sounds something like this:

So how are you feeling?

Tired.

You always say that.

You always say *that.*

I know. What kind of tired? Physical, emotional?

Physical. Not depressed.

Are you sure?

Yes. No anxiety. My self-esteem feels okay.

How does today feel to you?

Like a long one. Four clients this morning, five this afternoon. Then group.

You worried about group?

A little. My stomach just clinched a little when I thought of it.

What's that about?

X, I think. She's still mad at me. I'm waiting for it to come out.

Do you know how to respond when it does?

Sure. It's just her father shit getting triggered. I'll let her vent some, then point that out. Should be fine.

How's your stomach now?

Better. It unclenched.

And so on. Sometimes these talks turn into self-supervision sessions—i.e., helping myself solve clinical problems—but usually not. More often they provide what's called *self-soothing*. I use them to plan my day, identify feelings, solve problems, and generally settle myself down.

EXPLODING

Fritz Perls suggested that emotional health requires us to be able to explode in four ways: grief, anger, joy, and orgasm.[44]

To *explode* means to unleash your feelings, to express them without fear. It does *not* mean acting out destructively. I'm talking here about allowing your housebroken self—polite, careful, nervous, and self-conscious—to be momentarily swept away. To come down out of your head and *surrender* to feeling.

This doesn't mean being overwhelmed, either. You explode choicefully, so the real you can emerge. You choose to give up self-control.

If you can't explode, you implode. Most people are imploders:

normal socialized human beings trained to value self-control and restraint, not authenticity and certainly not explosion. Have you ever wondered why we call people we admire *cool* and people we disdain *assholes?* Cool people are neat; they contain everything. Assholes discharge shit. Shit's messy. We're trained to keep our shit together.

My work with imploders focuses mostly on undoing their emotional constipation. Some are mad and need a place to express their anger out loud without scaring people or being judged. Others are sad, stuck in mourning, discouraged or depressed, and need a place where they can stop putting a brave face on things.

And many are chronically scared from sitting on emotional shit so old they've forgotten where it came from. "It is not generally recognized that suppression of a feeling makes one afraid of that feeling," writes Alexander Lowen.[45] Having been scared shitless *(Keep it down in there)*, the fear of feeling itself forces them to continue holding in the very energy they need to let flow.

Many clients are afraid even to talk about feelings they've keep bottled for decades. Their anger or grief feels like a gorilla they keep chained in the basement and whose existence they're scared to acknowledge. It can take months to convince them *I'm* not scared of the gorilla, and then more months before they agree to crack the cellar door and take a look at it.

Others tell me they fear that if they start crying they won't be able to stop. "Sure you will," I say. "Eventually you'll have to pee and you'll stop for that. Or you'll get hungry and need a sandwich. Or you'll get tired and fall asleep. Not to worry." And that's how it goes.

I don't meet many people who don't need a good cry. Several good cries. They almost always feel better afterwards.

And then they often feel the need to apologize. Exploding in front of another person violates some deep-seated social more, triggering embarrassment or shame. I usually ignore the apology, pass them a tissue and congratulate them on getting their money's worth out of therapy. Then they laugh.

Finally, explosion can be life-saving.

> *A depressed client who's just discovered her husband's affair comes in and announces she wants to kill herself. I believe her; she has tried to before. I give her a piece of paper and a crayon and ask her to draw a cartoon of his face. She does. I tell her to label it with his name, and she does that. Then I have her place it on my hassock and hand her a tennis racquet I keep in my office. "Kill him," I say. She begins to beat the paper:* wahp, wahp, wahp. *"Harder," I say. "Tell him what you think of him." "You bastard," she cries, "I hate you, I trusted you, you lied to me, you broke my heart." The paper shreds into ribbons, then confetti. After five minutes she drops the racquet and sits, flushed and panting. I ask if she still wants to kill herself. "No," she says. "Now I want a fucking lawyer."*

PLAY

I often prescribe play to recovering clients.

"When was the last time you did something for fun?" I'll ask. "Not because it was good for you. Not because someone told you to. Not because it earned you money. Just because it felt good."

They usually reply with blank stares, like I've just lapsed into Bulgarian.

Few adults take play seriously. Artists do, as do some parents intent on really understanding their kids. But for the rest of us both the ability to play and to *value* play faded as we aged. Play came to seem at best pointless, and at worst irresponsible.

My dictionary defines *play* as "a recreational activity." An insipid definition, until you look twice at that second word.

Play is how we *recreate* ourselves.

It does this by providing a counterbalance to all the stuff that makes us sick, crazy, and addicted.

For example:

1. PLAY BALANCES LOSS OF SELF.

We are each torn between two impulses: self-gratification and the need to adapt. Much of this book has described how the latter impulse overwhelms us and coerces us into a life of compulsive control. Play counteracts this. It serves personal needs—self-expression, tension release, discharge of unruly impulses and feelings—without jeopardizing adaptation. We can be loud or exuberant or spontaneous or passionate or silly without scaring anyone or destabilizing the community. Play serves as a sort of safety valve for all these energies. When I play, I get the unhousebroken part of myself back.

2. PLAY BALANCES MONKEYMIND.

Monkeymind, remember, is that internal voice that severs us from reality by pinballing endlessly between memory and projection. Play stops this chatter by bringing us into the present. You can't play in the past or the future; you can only play here and now. Heraclitus wrote, "Time is a game played beautifully by children." Before monkeymind consumes them, kids play naturally, freely and without fear. Play offers one of the few respites from the scared maniac inhabiting your adult skull.

3. PLAY BALANCES NUMBNESS.

Earlier I described how we defend against anxiety by avoiding experience, resigning ourselves to thinking and stale familiarity instead. Play replaces this with pleasure. It matters little whether the play is public or private, causal or demanding, structured or wholly improvised: pleasure is inherent in play. Pleasure *defines* play. If you're not feeling pleasure, you're doing it wrong. And pleasure is essential. "Bodily pleasure is the source from which all our good feelings and good thinking stems," writes Alexander Lowen.

> If the bodily pleasure of an individual is destroyed, he becomes an angry, frustrated, and hateful person. His thinking becomes distorted, and his creative potential is lost. He develops self-destructive attitudes.[46]

We *need* pleasure. So we need play.

4. PLAY BALANCES THE NEED FOR CONTROL.

Finally, play teaches surrender. It is a form of nonattachment, letting go of goals and outcomes, a way of focusing on process instead of product. We play for its own sake, for how it feels, not what it leads to. In fact, we must let go of outcomes in order to play. To play *well* means not to accomplish something, but to enjoy yourself. To immerse yourself in experience. To lose your mind and come to your senses. To feel joy.

For control addicts, play is both the means of recovery and the whole point of recovering. When we play, we're recovering. And until we can play, we can't say we've recovered at all.

CREATIVITY

Penny is a painter, a careful, nervous one. Survivor of an abusive family that shut down all expressive outlets, she finds it difficult to talk. She can't relax or feel safe, not with me, not with herself. The therapy moves slowly. One day I ask to see her work. She shows me cell phone photos of careful landscapes and sedate bowls of fruit. All muted colors, all skillfully rendered, all dead.

"Want to try an experiment?" I ask.

I hand her a large pad of newsprint and an old box of Crayolas. "Don't talk," I say. "Take a deep breath. Close your eyes. Now imagine yourself as six years old. Remember being a six-year-old kid living in your parents' house. Remember what it sounded and felt like. Now draw what you're feeling. No figures or objects.

Lines, shapes, and colors only. And," I finish, "use your non-dominant hand."

She gives me a sharp look and I wait for her refusal. But she's braver than I'd guessed. She breathes in, closes her eyes. Then she takes a red crayon in her left hand and goes to work. She scribbles awkwardly and intently for 22 minutes. The result is an explosion on the page, a mishmash of vivid colors and vague forms fighting for dominance. She moves from one to the next to the next, frowning as if trying to hear directions from somewhere inside. The colors on the page seem to mirror the feelings in her face: angry reds, scared blacks, sad blues and purples. I'm projecting, I know. But it sure seems like that.

Finally the page is full. She stops and stares at what's she's made. "How do you feel?" I ask, but I know the answer.

"Like I threw up," she breathes.

We spend four weeks of sessions exploring this picture, which turns out to be nothing less than the emotional history of her childhood compressed onto a page.

Creative work is something else I prescribe to clients.

"Is there anything you like to do," I ask them, "or ever loved? Drawing or painting? Writing poetry or stories? Journaling? Haiku? Photography? Dancing? Crocheting? Inventing new chicken recipes? Making wind chimes out of sea shells? Anything?"

There's usually something they've done and loved. But their reply is invariably, "I'm not very good."

"Good's not the point," I say. "This is about creating a language, and finding a voice."

By *language* I mean a way to describe our inner experience. *Voice* means the courage to express personal truth.

These are not taught in schools. On the contrary. Like Penny, we are all survivors of an abusive family—if not a personal one, then the larger social one whose creatures we are. We cannot escape socialization and culture, which shape us into cogs within a particular social system, defined by the system's rules and values, dependent on its punishments and rewards.

If we want to be more than that, and if we want to escape the sickness that comes with over-adaptation, we must be creative.

Creative work is valuable to control addicts because it requires almost all the recovery practices described above—surrender and tolerance, detachment and faith, the ability to respond, the ability to play, healthy selfishness, pleasure, and both listening and talking to oneself

But beyond that, creativity is essential emotional work because it forces us to confront and define ourselves. Yes, we've each swallowed the poison pill. We're each split emotionally, struggle to accept ourselves, criticize and judge ourselves to excess. The difference between garden-variety neurotics and creative people is that creatives confront this condition directly. By risking creatively they face the demons inside, the ones hissing *don't say it* and *not good enough*. They feel fear and doubt, hear the hisses and take the risk anyway. They do it, in the end, as an act of courage and self-love.

So creative work is not just for artists. It represents, writes Rollo May, "the highest degree of emotional health, the expression of normal people in the act of actualizing themselves."[47]

THE KID IN THE CLOSET

There's no such thing as a grownup human being.

This is something you learn from doing psychotherapy.

Maybe the single most important something.

Each of us carries a kid inside, a part that never grows up. A part that stays tender, innocent, and vulnerable. Carl Jung wrote:

> In every adult there lurks a child—an eternal child, something that is always becoming, and calls for unceasing care, attention and education. That is the part of the personality which wants to develop and become whole.[48]

I half agree.

Yes, I see each client's Inner Kid less as the leading edge of personal growth. But as a practicing therapist I'm also forced to treat it as a collection of wounds.

Most adults are ashamed of the Kid. They perceive it as a weakness, a flaw or vulnerability. When the Kid makes an appearance—gets scared or cries, for example—they're embarrassed.

Shut up, they tell it. *You make me look ridiculous. Shut up and go away.*

This is no accident. It's the result of being parented by adults who largely forget what it felt like to be powerless, puzzled, and surrounded by giants. And of schools which cram kids into classrooms, ignore their needs for freedom, fresh air, and play, regiment their behavior and test them into obedience. All of this taught them *This is how you treat a kid.*

So naturally we end up doing the same thing to the Kid inside. As a result, most of us enter adulthood carrying a secret ragbag of unmet needs, unexpressed feelings, unresolved conflicts, and unhealed wounds.

We assume all this fear and pain is somehow our fault, a dirty secret. So we bury it, hide it even from ourselves for a long as we can. Many of us hide it until we become symptomatic: anxious, depressed, addicted, divorced.

Some end up in the office of someone like me, being told, in so many words, that they're guilty of Inner Child abuse. Because that's what it amounts to.

Hiding your Kid in the closet has the same effect as closeting a real child. So does telling the Kid *suck it up* or *behave yourself* or *stop acting like a baby*. It's disrespectful, hurtful, scary, and shaming. It doesn't make you stronger, braver, or tougher. It doesn't make you smarter or more adult.

It *does* guarantee you'll spend your so-called "adult years" feeling like a damaged Kid inside.

Recovery means reversing all this.

It means not just acknowledging the Kid, but befriending it.

It means learning to listen, and respect what we hear.

It means having the courage to live healthily selfish lives.

It means parenting ourselves better than our parents did.

There's no such thing as a grown-up person.

~ *Andre Malraux*

PRACTICING RESPONSIBILITY

Notes on practicing responsibility:

1. Your first act of responsibility is a conscious decision:

    From here on, I will take care of myself. I will listen for signs of what I need and respond accordingly whenever I can.

Don't skip this step. Write it down. Say it aloud. Share it with people you trust. It is necessary to counteract the secret decision you made long ago and have been acting out all these years: *I'll ignore myself. It's safer that way.*

2. Now focus on basic physical stuff. Eat when hungry, rest

when tired, pee when your bladder fills. Develop the courage to speak up for your physical needs when they make their presence known. Especially respect your need for rest. Stop running yourself ragged. Remember that "to do" lists are inherently endless. And that a nap is a beautiful thing.

3. Move on to emotional needs. Practice noticing when you feel angry or frightened, lonely or hurt. Use four words to start naming your feelings: *mad, sad, glad, scared*. Practice identifying the physical signs that signal the presence of these feelings: tense shoulders, tight stomach, ache in your heart. Become someone who, when asked *How are you feeling?*, has a real answer to give.

4. Now attend to your social needs, your boundaries. Notice who you like and who you don't. You may have been faking it for so long you've forgotten. Pay attention now. Notice whose presence makes you uncomfortable and whose presence allows you to relax and feel safe. Trust your gut and respect your preferences. Then, to the extent you can, spend less time with the uncomfortable group and more time with the group where you can be yourself.

5. Finally, practice telling others what you feel. This step takes preparation, since you need safe relationships in order to complete it. It also brings us to the part of Plan B called *intimacy*, which I discuss in the chapters ahead. For now, just remember that recovery in isolation isn't recovery at all, just a new version of your defensive Plan A. Be brave and trust the words of Anton Chekhov: "You must trust and believe in people, or life becomes impossible."

INTIMACY

Finally, the third alternative.

Intimacy is the ability to be yourself with other people, and to allow them to do the same with you.

Intimacy is the *interpersonal* alternative to compulsive control. Surrender, the *spiritual* alternative, corrects how we relate to the universe. Responsibility, the *emotional* alternative, corrects how we relate to ourselves. Intimacy is the alternative that helps us correct our relationship to other people.

It is the means to real connection, healthy communication, and genuine love.

It's also the most difficult of the three practices. There are two good reasons for this:

First, it requires we learn and practice the other alternatives as well. To be intimate with another person you must first *surrender* control over that person—which includes not controlling what they think of or feel towards you—and then *respond* to them as honestly as possible. For control addicts, that's like learning to play violin while ice skating.

Second, intimacy can be frightening. It means dropping our defenses, letting ourselves feel intensely, and risking rejection and other emotional injuries. That's hard for anyone. But if you've been traumatized by relationships in the past, the very idea of such vulnerability can be paralyzing.

So the first question to ask is: Why bother?

WHY BOTHER?

Sadly, most of us don't.

Most people I meet have been so wounded in relationships that they're afraid to trust them again. They've decided feeling and vulnerability are just too damned dangerous. So they stay in hiding and, around other people, they armor up.

It's how they became control addicts, and why they remain so.

Others are forced to learn intimacy in order to recover from some illness that's even scarier. Recovering alcoholics learn to stand in meetings and share painful secrets, and depressives learn to express feelings in a therapy group. Hard work, yes. But they do it because they know that the alternative is even harder.

There are some people, though, who set out to learn this most challenging of skills because they understand that intimacy is as good as it gets; that for human beings, nothing in life is as rewarding, nurturing, healing, or strengthening as a truly intimate relationship.

Yale researcher Robert E. Lane conducted an exhaustive study to find out what really makes people happy, publishing his findings as a book titled *The Loss of Happiness in Market Democracies*. What makes people happy? Not money, Lane reports:

> We get happiness primarily from people: it is their affection or dislike, their good or bad opinion of us, their acceptance or rejection that most influence our moods. Income is mostly sought in the service of these forms of social esteem, as Adam Smith reported long ago.[49]

Unfortunately most of us don't realize this. "People are not very good judges of how, even within the private spheres of their lives, to increase let alone maximize their happiness,"[50] Lane writes. So we pursue the wrong goals: money, success, possessions, status, individualism, distraction, and, yes, control.

> My hypothesis is that there is a kind of famine of warm interpersonal relationships, of easy-to-reach neighbors, of encircling, inclusive memberships, and of solidary family life...It has been said, therefore, that the United States is not as happy as it is rich. Something has gone wrong. The economy that made Americans both rich and happy at one point in history is misleading them, is offering more

money, which does not make them happier, instead of more companionship, which probably would.[51]

This means our unhappiness, like our craving for control, is a cultural phenomenon, not just a personal one. If we want to be happier we must find ways to detach from the culture that has led us astray. One way is to shift our priorities and pay more attention to the quality of our relationships, since, it appears, we cannot be happier or healthier than those relationships are.

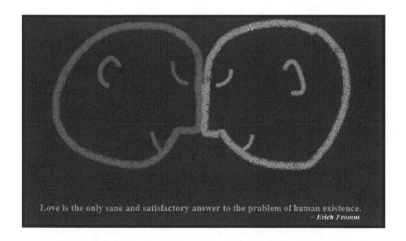

Love is the only sane and satisfactory answer to the problem of human existence.
— *Erich Fromm*

TALK

Intimacy depends on the quality of communication.

The first step to raising that quality?

Not doing what we normally do.

The psychologist Thomas Gordon once identified 12 "roadblocks to communication" between parents and children.[52] It's a good list to memorize, since each item is essentially a controlling behavior capable of destroying intimacy between anyone and anyone else:

1. Ordering or directing

2. Warning or threatening

3. Advising or suggesting

4. Arguing or persuading

5. Lecturing or moralizing

6. Criticizing, judging, or blaming

7. Agreeing or praising

8. Ridiculing or shaming

9. Analyzing or diagnosing

10. Reassuring or sympathizing

11. Questioning or probing

12. Withdrawing, humoring, or distracting

A client with whom I shared this list replied, "What does that leave? Hand signals?"

I sympathize. We're so used to these ways of unconsciously controlling each other that it's hard to imagine doing without them.

But there are healthier ways to talk.

I-STATEMENTS

The first way to learn is *I-statements*.

Have you ever noticed how sentences containing the word "you" tend to make the listener defensive or angry? I-statements avoid this by focusing on the speaker instead.

Compare:

YOU-STATEMENT	I-STATEMENT
You're a jerk.	I'm mad at you.
You're not making sense.	I'm confused.

You shouldn't do that.	I'm uncomfortable with your behavior.
You look pissed.	I'm scared of you.
Are you okay?	I'm worried about you.
You look great.	I'm attracted to you.

Imagine yourself on the receiving end of the first list of statements. Now imagine hearing the second list. Which do you think would lead to better communication?

Three things to remember about I- and you-statements:

1. UNDERLYING MOTIVE

Note that not all you-statements include the word *you*. The real difference between You-statements and I-statements has less to do with the words they contain than with the motives behind them. You-statements are meant to *conceal* the speaker's thoughts or feelings by directing attention elsewhere. Common ways to do this include questioning, criticizing, intellectualizing, advising, and blaming. All these are much safer to say than they are to hear.

2. SOCIAL COURAGE

I-statements, on the other hand, reveal the speaker. Since it brings him or her out of hiding, each I-statement represents something of a risk, an experiment in vulnerability. So I-statements require some guts to make. Rollo May calls this *social courage:*

> ...the courage to relate to other human beings, the capacity to risk one's self in the hope of achieving meaningful intimacy. It is the courage to invest one's self over a period of time in a relationship that will demand an increasing openness.[53]

3. DISGUISED YOU-STATEMENTS

Once in a group where we were practicing I-statements, one member turned to another and said, "I feel you're lying." The woman to whom she was speaking frowned, then turned to me and asked, "Was that really an I-statement?"

No, it wasn't. It's what I call a *disguised* you-statement. It only pretends to reveal something about the speaker; its real subject—or target—is the other person. It's a sort of sneak attack. (The listener knew this because it left her feeling hurt.) The I-statement behind it was probably something like *I don't like you* or *I don't trust you* or *I'm mad at you because I think you're lying.*

You can evaluate such statements by asking yourself one simple question: "Did it tell me what the speaker is feeling inside?" I-statements allow you to answer Yes. You-statements leave you still in the dark.

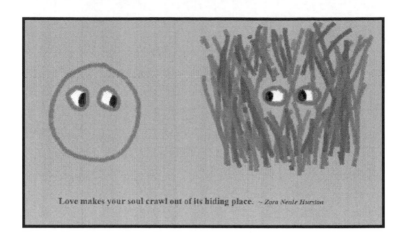

Love makes your soul crawl out of its hiding place. ~ *Zora Neale Hurston*

FEEDBACK

Then there's *feedback*, which I teach in therapy groups.

Group requires a lot of emotional safety and feedback was created to maximize that. Say a group member describes a fight with her husband. I'll ask the other members: "What were you feeling or remembering while you listened to that story? Or what are you feeling right now?"

Feedback is the sharing of such personal reactions and associations. It does not include opinion, criticism, judgment, diagnosis, or advice. It sounds like this:

> *I feel angry. Her husband reminds me of my husband, and why I divorced the selfish son of a bitch.*

I feel anxious. The story scared me. I hate conflict. It reminds me of growing up with parents who fought all the time.

I'm feeling sad. I like X, and didn't realize she was unhappily married.

I feel bored. I've heard too many of these stories lately. All my friends seem to be married to jerks.

And so on.

In group the benefits of feedback are many. It creates safety by allowing members to share personal experience without fear of unsolicited comments or advice. It helps them know each other emotionally by identifying experiences and feelings they share. It also turns a group of strangers into a community. Feedback is a sort of gift members give one another, a gesture of openness and goodwill.

I would not mention feedback here, though, if it was useful only in therapy groups. I teach it to all of my clients as an important intimacy skill.

Its main value is that it helps us better understand the roots of our deepest reactions to other people.

Recall chapter 32, where I defined transference as what happens when one relationship feels like another. This experience is more common than we realize. I believe that whenever we have strong emotional reactions—for example, immediately like or dislike someone we've just met—the strength comes from some memory that person triggers. Feedback is a way of flushing out those memories.

I teach feedback by asking clients to translate interpersonal experiences using this format:

When you [A], I feel [B], because [C].

"[A] is the other person's behavior," I explain. "Whatever they did or said to trigger your reaction. [B] is whatever feeling came up: *mad, sad, glad, scared*, or some form of one of those. And [C] is where that feeling came from."

Sample ABC statements:

When you [A] talk about leaving group, I feel [B] angry, because [C] so many people have walked out on me.

When you raise your voice, I feel scared, because in my family angry people usually got violent.

When you interrupt me, I feel sad and discouraged, because all my life no one ever listened to me.

Identifying [C] can be tricky, since often we don't know why we feel what we feel. I tell clients not to worry about that: "Just leave [C] blank. Finish with *and I don't know why*." Regular practice of feedback often leads them to memories which explain why they feel what they feel.

I suggest clients start by ABCing their experiences internally.

Later on they can graduate to sharing with people important to them.

I don't usually recommend using feedback with everyone out in the world. But occasionally my clients do, with interesting results.

> A week after we review the ABC format in group, one member, a retail store manager, comes in looking pleased with herself. "I ABC'd an employee today," she announces. "I told her that when I try to help her with problems and she gets all defensive, I feel frustrated, because it's like she doesn't get I'm only trying to help." "Wow," says another member. "What did she say?" "She apologized. I've known her a year, and she's never apologized before. Then," she grins, "she told me how her mom's always telling her how stupid she is. She basically ABC'd me back." The group applauds.

MONOLOGUING

Finally, *monologuing* is a practice I teach couples who want to learn intimate communication.

It's a simple procedure. The couple sits together and take turns sharing (a) what they resent and (b) what they appreciate about each other. Each partner speaks for five minutes only.

For example, the first partner may start off with something like:

> *I resent it when you comment on my weight.*

> *I resent your not getting off the phone when I come home.*

> *I resent your monopolizing the remote when we watch TV together.*

I resent your leaving newspapers on the bed.

I resent that your friends stay in touch with you and mine never call me.

Throughout this the other partner just sits and listens—no interrupting, questions, explanations or comments. (With one exception. See below.) After the first partner is done listing resentments, he or she concludes with appreciations:

I appreciate your returning my library book.

I appreciate that you defend me when my mother criticizes my parenting.

I appreciate that you apologized for hurting my feelings.

I appreciate it when you compliment my cooking.

I appreciate how you laugh at my jokes.

It is essential during monologuing to make only I-statements (*I resent this* and *I appreciate that*) and to avoid all you-statements (like *You always* or *You never* or *You jerk*). This is so important that if one partner does slip into you-statements— which happens easily, especially in the beginning—the other is permitted to point it out and request I-statements instead. That's the only exception to the no-interruption rule

Since this structured exercise is so different from the talking most couples have been doing, they usually have lots of questions. Like:

Why are I-statements so important?

Because You-statements are experienced by your partner as an attack. They provoke defensiveness and conflict instead of communication and closeness. And the goal here is to leave you feeling closer.

What if I have an issue too big to resolve in only five minutes?

You don't monologue to resolve issues. You monologue to get in touch with each other's feelings—to share emotional information, not settle disputes.

Why can't I interrupt if I don't like what I'm hearing?

Because monologuing is not arguing. It's an *alternative* to arguing—a way to vent feelings in a safe place, knowing you'll be listened to, and without having to worry about being attacked or starting a fight. The goal here is communication, not competition.

But what if what I hear upsets me?

One goal of monologuing is to teach you to listen *nondefensively*—that is, without taking your partner's feelings personally. We can't choose what we feel. Feelings aren't right or wrong, they just are. Our only choice is between holding them in (which tends to make us sick) or sharing them.

Monologues create a safe and respectful space in which to share them with each other.

But what if I'm still upset after we finish?

Sure, that's possible. If it happens, give yourself a day to cool down. Marinate what you heard. Your reaction may well change over time. If you're still upset, you can always bring any unresolved feelings to the next monologuing session.

Why do we share resentments first?

Because resentments tend to block all other feelings. Once they're out of the way, it's easier to express positive feelings like affection and gratitude. And ending your monologue with appreciations reaffirms the basic connection between you and your partner. It reminds you why you're together in the first place.

Some of my resentments seem petty even to me.

Is it really necessary to talk about such things?

Yes. Unexpressed resentments don't just vanish; they go into hiding. Then they collect, to where one or both of you starts looking (consciously or unconsciously) for a fight. Monologuing relieves this tension in small doses, so major battles become less likely. Think of it as pulling emotional weeds before they can overrun your garden.

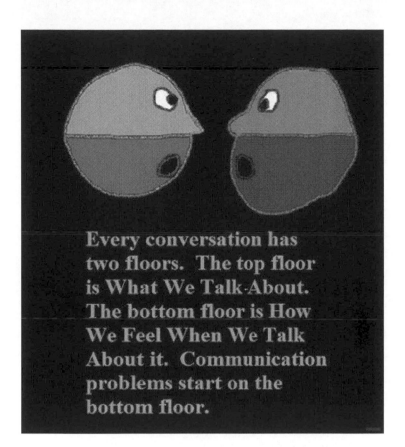

Every conversation has two floors. The top floor is What We Talk-About. The bottom floor is How We Feel When We Talk About it. Communication problems start on the bottom floor.

WITHOUT TALK

But some couples can't talk.

Can't talk, that is, without getting into trouble. For them talk is inseparable from problem solving, which is inseparable from arguing, which inevitably triggers old rage and reopens old wounds. They cannot talk to each other without blaming, accusing, attacking, complaining, or invalidating what the other thinks or feels.

This is more common than it sounds. It's why I begin all my couples counseling by seeing each partner alone for a while. Stressed couples need this time to get to know and trust me, to feel safe and understood. Skipping or skimping on this first step usually leads to their repeating, on my sofa, the same arguments they have at home.

But sometimes no preparation can get them communicating peaceably. Individual work and all attempts at teaching I-statements, feedback and monologuing fail. That leaves nothing but nonverbal communication.

"How's your sex life?" I ask.

Often the answer is: surprisingly good. Some couples consider sex so important that they've found ways to put down their weapons when they go to bed.

If that's the case, I say "Good. Then stop trying to talk for a while. Have more sex instead."

They usually laugh with relief. And often this prescription is just the thing to get them unstuck. It builds on something they're already good at and so gives them confidence. It removes the temptation to use withholding sex as a punishment (*Hey, Steve told us to do this*). It reduces the tension between them, softens their anger and resistance. Then I can resume trying to teach them how to talk.

If for some reason more sex is contraindicated, I'll recommend cuddling, if cuddling is something they enjoy. Or dancing. Or taking walks together holding hands. Or cooking together, gardening together, or exercising the dog. Or sitting on the same sofa, each reading their own book. All without talking.

I call this talking without talking, because it involves an exchange of important messages:

I'm still here.

I still care about you.

You can feel safe with me.

I can hold my fire.

PRACTICING INTIMACY

One last word about intimacy:

Most people are terribly confused about relationships, especially those involving love.

Partly this is because relationship itself makes seemingly impossible demands, like the need to be connected and separate at the same time.

Partly it's because we lack healthy models while growing up, or are traumatized by seeing how destructive really bad relationships can be.

Partly it's because we each bring a wounded Kid to adult relationships, unconsciously expecting our partner to meet all the Kid's needs and heal all its wounds, and then feel betrayed and enraged when they cannot.

And partly it's because of all the myths and fantasies we absorb about romantic love, true love, perfect love, deathless passion, and soul mates.

Personally, I believe the main reason we struggle with relationship is that it kicks the crap out of the illusion of control.

I was reminded of this yesterday at the park. I was with my grandson, a friendly two-and-a-half-year-old. I watched him approach two bigger boys and chirp "Hi." I watched the boys ignore him and turn away. I watched his eyes cloud over. It felt like an arrow entering my heart.

You can't love and feel in control. You can't help but feel hostage to the feelings and fortunes of someone you love. Nor can you avoid frustration, disappointment, confusion, conflict, rejection, abandonment or loss. Love makes you vulnerable to all these. That's just the cost of doing business. Love always involves hurt.

The solution, to the extent we have one, is not to avoid love or attachment, but to become less controlling in how we love.

We must learn to try not to make our relationships predictable, orderly or safe. To give up expectations instead, and accept the flawed, needy people we love; to accept and express the flawed, needy people we *are*. That's the whole point of intimacy. And intimacy is as good as human relationship gets.

STAGES OF RECOVERY

Control addicts go through four fairly predictable stages in recovery.

STAGE 1: ENMESHMENT

This is the Plan A stage, where the addict still feels and functions like a powerless child. It's the stage of blurred boundaries and compulsive controlling. Unable to distinguish external triggers from her internal reactions, she tries constantly to control people, places and things, and becomes anxious or depressed when she can't. It's as if those externals are attached by electric wires to her brain, and any upset *out there* causes emotional distress *in here*. This is the stage at which most clients enter therapy, with no clear idea of what's hurting them or why they're so miserable most of the time.

STAGE 2: DETACHMENT

Here the addict begins to identify her triggers and to step back from them. She learns to notice *that* she's controlling and *when* she's controlling. She gets better at distinguishing Mine from Not Mine. She learns to listen to her body, identify her needs, and to practice self-care. She begins to get more rest, say No more often, seek emotional support, and make herself a priority. The results are a sense of relief, hope, and freedom. Life starts to feel easier.

STAGE 3: NARCISSISM

Here the addict's emotional pendulum swings to the other extreme from where she began, and she moves into a phase of adolescent self-absorption. She's so determined to take better care of herself that she goes overboard. She can be selfish, stubborn or insensitive, may overindulge in alcohol or drugs or sex. This stage can be uncomfortable for the other people in her life. But it's a necessary corrective to all the years she spent hiding out. And it's usually temporary, just as adolescence is. At this point, some clients feel the need to rebel against me, even to leave therapy. When this happens, I usually just let them go. Their decision is premature; they still have growing up to do. I can only hope they'll come back when they realize it. Some do, some don't. Clients who remain in therapy move faster into Stage 4.

STAGE 4: MUTUALITY

Here the addict grows out of second adolescence and begins practicing more mature skills. Her self-acceptance is quieter now; she no longer needs to trumpet who she is. She's good at trusting and taking care of herself. She makes I-statements easily, and appreciates the I-statements of others. She's better at accepting both their limitations and her own. Most importantly, she's come to redefine what "healthy relationship" means to her. She understands *mutuality*, the conviction that what's good for another is good for her. She sees healthy relationship as collaboration, not competition. Basketball coach Phil Jackson once observed that "The strength of the team is each individual member, and the strength of each member is the team." In Stage 4, the addict finally sees that a relationship is only as strong as each partner, and each partner is only as strong as the relationship.

LOPSIDED

Because men and women tend to be emotionally lopsided, their recoveries tend to be lopsided, too.

Lopsided means unbalanced. Most of us are raised lopsided.

(Here follows some broad generalizations based on my professional experience. To the extent that your experience differs, feel free to reject any or all of them.)

Most men are raised to function as machines. Most women are raised to function as hostages.

Men are taught to sacrifice their emotional selves. Women are taught to sacrifice their independence and autonomy.

Men are expected to be tough, brave, and self-reliant. Women are expected to be endlessly accepting, sensitive, and giving.

> *I'm eight years old when I go to sleepaway camp. On my first night I'm lonely and homesick. I ask the camp director if I can call home. He refuses. "You're a big boy now. When you're in the army you won't be able to call your mother."*

> *I'm nine years old and Mom is fed up with parenting: "I'm sorry I ever had a daughter." She packs my clothes in a suitcase, puts it on the front porch, and tells me to leave. Hysterical, I go to Dad. "Now, now," he frowns. "Have some patience. Mommy's just having a bad day."*

Men are taught to stuff their feelings and work hard. Women are taught to stuff their feelings and give until it hurts.

Men are taught to value success out in the world and to judge themselves according to how well they're doing at work. Women are taught to value the approval of others and to judge themselves according to how their personal relationships are going.

Both are trained—by family, school and workplace—to conceal what they really need and who they really are for the sake of these gender-specific social roles.

Both end up suffering in fairly predictable ways.

> *My typical male client has been following the male Plan A for decades. He comes into therapy angry, anxious, depressed and/or*

addicted, unsure who he really is and what he really wants, and wondering why years of Big Boy hard work and self-sacrifice have left him feeling so lonely, empty, and inadequate

My typical female client has been trained to be codependent—to lose herself in relationships by putting the needs and feelings of others ahead of her own. She comes into therapy guilty, anxious, depressed and/or addicted, unsure who she really is or what she really wants, and wondering why years of being a Good Girl haven't left her feeling valued, appreciated, and loved.

So both men and women end up lopsided. And both usually need some help to overcome their conditioning and create lives that are more balanced.

For men the most difficult and important task of recovery is regaining the ability to feel. Their therapy focuses first on understanding the function of feelings, then on unearthing feelings they buried long ago, then expressing them in healthy ways, integrating them into their important relationships, and finally using them as a basis for making decisions and life choices.

For women, the most difficult and important task is developing the strength and courage to detach, especially from others' expectations. They generally find it easier to identify and express what they feel. But they struggle with believing their feelings are as valid and important as the feelings of the other people in their lives. They also tend to have blurred boundaries, to confuse the needs and problems of others with their own. Therapeutic work with such women often involves reminding them, over and over, of who they are and who they are not.

Let's be clear. No matter how hard we work in recovery, some lopsidedness is finally inescapable, just as is some addiction to control.

But we can regain much of our balance. We can reclaim abandoned parts of who we are.

Which, after all, is what *recover* means: to get something back, to reclaim what we lost.

Life is not orderly. No matter how we try to make life so, right in the middle of it we die, lose a leg, fall in love, drop a jar of applesauce.

~ Natalie Goldberg

SOBER

The goal of recovering from addiction to a substance like alcohol is called sobriety. As every recovering addict knows, *sober* means more than abstinence. Sure, you stop using. But you also grow up.

Growing beyond control addiction means experiencing a sea change in your point of view. "I once heard a sober alcoholic say that drinking never made him happy, but it made him feel like he was going to be happy in about fifteen minutes," writes Heather King.[54] A nice summary of addiction, that. It also points us towards a sober view of control.

Sober means learning to accept where you are and stop wishing for elsewhere. You stop fighting reality. You declare peace with what is, right here and right now. And you stay receptive to what's going to happen next.

From this declared peace stems, at least in theory, all the good things of life: self-acceptance, realistic problem-solving, successful relationships, genuine love, gratitude, and the closest anyone ever comes to peace of mind.

But let's face it: recovery—like growing up—is hard work. It takes practice, patience, and courage, and most of us commit to it only when we're left with no other choice.

Still, the rewards are worth noting.

My own recovery work has left me more patient, less antsy. I do better in traffic jams and on long bank lines. I'm less apt to take things personally, or be irritated by people like slow waiters or dumb politicians. I'm quicker to catch myself when I do get impatient, pissy or defensive. At the same time I'm less scared to ask people for what I want or tell them what I really think. I'm more direct with my clients. I make more money than I used to because I stopped being afraid to raise my fees. I also notice greater stamina, more tolerance for discomfort and stress. I can work longer and with more focus than I have in thirty years. But now, when I stop working, I stop working. Well, no, not always. My wife stills sees me as a workaholic, which must mean I still am. But I experience myself differently inside. I can see overworking as a problem now. And I'm able to detach long enough to visit the park with my grandson, eat tacos with my son, or watch *Scandal* with my wife. Monkeymind no longer fills every nook and cranny in my head. The thing I like most about needing less control, though, is how it's left me with a lower center of gravity. Things that once tipped me over into anxiety or rage no longer can. I can better tolerate delay and disappointment and ambiguity and the unpredictable and the unexpected.

During a routine physical my doc runs a cardiogram and finds a blip that suggests a TIA (transient ischemic attack). He tells me to drive to the ER. I feel fine, but I go. At the hospital they put me on a gurney and park me in a hallway for four hours while they run tests. I have to cancel six sessions, calm my worried wife over the phone, wonder what all this is costing me, and then just lie there and wait. At one time I would have reacted to all this with frustration, worry, or anger. Now I surprise myself by closing my eyes and taking a nap.

THE LAST FREEDOM

In 1942 psychiatrist Viktor Frankl was arrested by the Nazis and imprisoned in four concentration camps over three years. He later wrote:

> We who lived in concentration camps can remember the men who walked through the huts comforting others, giving away their last piece of bread. They may have been few in number, but they offer sufficient proof that everything can be taken from a man but one thing: the last of the human freedoms—to choose one's attitude in any given set of circumstances, to choose one's own way.[55]

No, we can't stop wanting control.

But we can stop wanting it as much, seeking it everywhere,

and feeling scared when it cannot be found. We can grow up, become powerful, and create lives centered around other things. Real things. We can switch our focus from externals to how we respond to those externals. We can choose our own way.

We can do that. You can do that.

For those who decide to reach for life beyond control, I offer this reassurance from the *Tao te ching*:

> *Do you want to improve the world?*
> *I don't think it can be done.*
>
> *The world is sacred.*
> *It can't be improved.*
> *If you tamper with it, you'll ruin it.*
> *If you treat it like an object, you'll lose it.*
>
> *There is a time for being ahead,*
> *a time for being behind;*
> *a time for being in motion,*
> *a time for being at rest;*
> *a time for being vigorous,*
> *a time for being exhausted;*
> *a time for being safe,*
> *a time for being in danger.*
>
> *The Master sees things as they are,*
> *without trying to control them.*
> *She lets them go their own way,*
> *and resides at the center of the circle.*[56]

Sometimes I go about pitying myself, and all the while, a great wind carries me across the sky. ~ *Ojibway saying*

NOTES

1. Judith Lewis Herman, *Trauma and Recovery* (New York: Basic Books, 1992), 33.

2. Peter A. Levine, *Waking the Tiger: Healing Trauma* (Berkeley, CA: North Atlantic Books, 1997), 53-54.

3. Alexander Lowen, *Depression and the Body: The Biological Basis of Faith and Reality* (New York: Penguin Arkana, 1972), 27-28.

4. Quoted in *Psychotherapy East and West* by Alan Watts (New York: Ballantine Books, 1961).

5. Sidney M. Jourard, *The Transparent Self* (New York: D. Van Nostrand, 1971), 6.

6. David Viscott, *The Language of Feelings* (New York: Pocket Books, 1977), 9.

7. Viscott, *op. cit.*, 9.

8. Philip Yancey & Dr. Paul Brand, *The Gift of Pain: Why We Hurt and What We Can Do About It* (Grand Rapids, MI: Zondervan Publishing House, 1993), 58.

9. Frederick S. Perls, *In and Out of the Garbage Pail* (New York: Bantam Books, 1969), 9.

10. James E. Miller, *Word, Self, Reality: The Rhetoric of Imagination* (New York: Dodd, Mead 1972), 2.

11. Joseph Campbell, *The Power of Myth* (New York: Doubleday, 1988), 146.

12. Frederick S. Perls, *In and Out of the Garbage Pail* (New York: Bantam Books, 1969), 36.

13. Alexander Lowen, *Fear of Life* (New York: Collier Books, 1980), 2.

14. Shauna Niequist, *Cold Tangerines: Celebrating the Extraordinary Nature of Everyday Life* (Grand Rapids, MI: Zondervan, 2007), 74.

15. Dalai Lama, *The Art of Happiness* (New York: Riverhead Books, 1998), 7.

16. Webster's New Collegiate Dictionary (Springfield, MA: G. & C. Merriam Company, 1977), 830.

17. Paul Foxman, *Dancing with Fear: Overcoming Anxiety in a World of Stress and Uncertainty* (Northvale NJ: Jason Aronson, 1996), 48.

18. Alexander Lowen, *The Spirituality of the Body* (New York: Macmillan, 1990), 45.

19. Frederick S. Perls, *Gestalt Therapy Verbatim* (Layfayette, CA: Real People Press, 1969), 178.

20. Stephen Cope, *The Wisdom of Yoga: A Seeker's Guide to Extraordinary Living* (New York: Bantam Books, 2006), 136.

21. Judith Viorst, *Imperfect Control: Our Lifelong Struggles with Power and Surrender* (New York: Simon & Schuster, 1998), 13.

22. Violet Weingarten, *Intimations of Mortality* (New York: Alfred A. Knopf, 1978), 87.

23. Mark Epstein, *Going to Pieces Without Falling Apart: A Buddhist Perspective on Wholeness* (New York: Broadway Books, 1998), 120.

24. Mark Epstein, *Thoughts Without a Thinker* (New York: Basic Books, 1995), 40.

25. Chogyam Trungpa, *Cutting through Spiritual Materialism* (Boston, MA: Shambhala Publications, 1973), 58.

26. Charlotte Joko Beck, *Everyday Zen: Love and Work* (New York: Harper & Row, 1989), 5.

27. Stephanie Brown, *Treating the Alcoholic: A Developmental Model of Recovery* (New York: John Wiley & Sons, 1985), 15-16.

28. Mark Epstein, *Thoughts Without a Thinker* (New York: Basic Books, 1995), 86-7.

29. Ralph Keyes, *The Courage to Write: How Writers Transcend Fear* (New York: Henry Holt & Company, 1995), 138.

30. Alan Watts, *The Wisdom of Insecurity: A Message for the Age of Anxiety* (New York: Vintage Books, 1951), 90.

31. Anne Lamott, *Bird by Bird: Some Instructions on Writing and Life* (New York: Anchor Books, 1994), 29-30.

32. Tara Brach, *Radical Acceptance: Embracing Your Life with the Heart of a Buddha* (New York: Bantam Books, 2003), 15-17.

33. Frederick Perls, *Gestalt Therapy Verbatim* (Lafayette, CA: Real People Press, 1969), 18.

34. William James, *The Varieties of Spiritual Experience: A Study in Human Nature* (New York: New American Library, 1958), 59

35. David Mamet, *The Verdict* (1982). Often attributed to the Bible, where it does not appear.

36. Susan Salzberg, *Faith: Trusting Your Own Deepest Experience* (New York: Riverhead Books, 2002), 12.

37. James 2:26, *The Holy Bible, Standard Edition* (New York: Thomas Nelson & Sons, 1901), 254.

38. *Webster's New World Dictionary, Second College Edition* (New York: Simon & Schuster, 1980), 1292.

39. *Roget's International Thesaurus* (New York: Thomas Y. Crowell Company, 1946), 643.

40. Dorothy Corkille Brigs, *Your Child's Self-Esteem: The Key to Life* (New York: Dolphin Books, 1975), 3-4.

41. Wayne Muller, *Legacy of the Heart: The Spiritual Advantages of a Painful Childhood* (New York: Simon & Schuster, 1992), 103.

42. Alexander Lowen, *Depression and the Body: The Biological Basis of Faith and Reality* (New York: Penguin Arkana, 1972), 12.

43. Frederick S. Perls, *Gestalt Therapy Verbatim* (Lafayette, CA: Real People Press, 1969), 63.

44. Fritz Perls, *Gestalt Therapy Verbatim* (Lafayette, CA: Real People Press, 1969), 56.

45. Alexander Lowen, *The Spirituality of the Body* (New York: Macmillan, 1990), 45.

46. Alexander Lowen, *Pleasure: A Creative Approach to Life* (New York: Penguin Books, 1970), 15.

47. Rollo May, *The Courage to Create* (New York: W.W. Norton & Company, 1975), 40.

48. Carl Jung, *Collected Works of C.G. Jung, Volume 17: The Development of Personality* (Princeton, NJ: Princeton University Press, 1954), 286.

49. Robert E. Lane, *The Loss of Happiness in Market Democracies* (New Haven, NJ: Yale University Press, 2000), 9-10.

50. Lane *op. cit.*, 6.

51. Lane, *op. cit.*, 9-10.

52. Thomas E. Gorden, *P.E.T.: Parent Effectiveness Training* (New York: Three Rivers Press, 1970), 103.

53. Rollo May, *The Courage to Create* (New York: W.W. Norton & Company, 1975), 17.

54. Heather King, *Parched: A Memoir* (New York: Penguin, 2005), 141.

55. Viktor E. Frankl, *Man's Search for Meaning: An Introduction to Logotherapy* (New York: Washington Square Press, 1963), 104.

56. Lao-tzu, *Tao te ching*, trans Stephen Mitchell (New York: HarperPerennial, 1991), verse 29.

BIBLIOGRAPHY

Beck, Charlotte Joko. *Everyday Zen: Love and Work*. New York: Harper & Row, 1989.

Briggs, Dorothy Corkille. *Your Child's Self-Esteem: The Key to Life*. New York: Dolphin Books, 1975.

Brown, Stephanie. *Treating the Alcoholic: A Developmental Model of Recovery*. New York: John Wiley & Sons, 1985.

Brown, Stephanie. *Treating Adult Children of Alcoholics: A Developmental Perspective*. New York: John Wiley & Sons, 1988.

Campbell, Joseph with Bill Moyers. *The Power of Myth*. New York: Doubleday, 1986.

Conger, John P. *The Body in Recovery: Somatic Psychotherapy and the Self.* Berkeley, CA: Frog, Ltd., 1994.

Cope, Stephen. *The Wisdom of Yoga: A Seeker's Guide to Extraordinary Living.* New York: Bantam, 2006.

Csikszmentmihalyi, Mihaly. *Flow: The Psychology of Optimal Experience.* New York: HarperPerennial, 1990.

Donaldson-Pressman, Stephanie and Robert M. Pressman. *The Narcissistic Family: Diagnosis and Treatment.* San Francisco: Jossey-Bass, 1994.

Dalai Lama & Howard C. Cutler. *The Art of Happiness: A Handbook for Living.* New York: Riverhead Books, 1998.

Epstein, Mark. *Thoughts Without a Thinker: Psychotherapy from a Buddhist Perspective.* New York: Basic Books, 1995.

Epstein, Mark. *Going to Pieces without Falling Apart: A Buddhist Perspective on Wholeness.* New York: Broadway Books, 1998.

Epstein, Mark. *Going on Being: Buddhism and the Way of Change.* New York: Broadway Books, 2001.

Epstein, Mark. *Open to Desire: Embracing a Lust for Life—Insights from Buddhism & Psychotherapy.* New York: Gotham Books, 2005.

Fields, Rick with Peggy Taylor, Rex Weyler, and Rick Ingrassi. *Chop Wood, Carry Water: A Guide to Finding Spiritual Fulfillment in Everyday Life.* New York: Jeremy P. Tarcher, 1984.

Foxman, Paul. *Dancing with Fear: Overcoming Anxiety in a World of Stress and Uncertainty*. Northvale, NJ: Jason Aaronson, 1996.

Frankl, Viktor E. *Man's Search for Meaning: An Introduction to Logotherapy*. New York: Washington Square Press, 1963.

Freud, Sigmund. *Civilization and its Discontents*. New York: W.W. Norton & Company, 1961.

Fritz, Robert. *The Path of Least Resistance: Learning to Become the Creative Force in Your Own Life*. New York: Fawcett Columbine, 1984.

_____. *Creating*. New York: Fawcett Columbine, 1991.

Gordon, Thomas. *Parent Effectiveness Training*. New York: Three Rivers Press, 1970.

LeLoup, Jean-Yves. *The Gospel of Thomas: The Gnostic Wisdom of Jesus*. Rochester, VT: Inner Traditions, 2005.

Herman, Judith. *Trauma and Recovery*. New York: Basic Books, 1992.

Hillman, James. *Kinds of Power: A guide to its Intelligent Uses*. New York: Doubleday, 1995.

James, William. *The Varieties of Spiritual Experience: A Study in Human Nature*. New York: New American Library, 1958.

Jourard, Sidney. *The Transparent Self*. New York: D. Van Nostrand, 1971.

Jung, Carl G. *Collected Works of C.G. Jung, Volume 17: The Develop-ment of Personality.* Princeton, NJ: Princeton University Press, 1954.

Keyes, Ralph. *The Courage to Write: How Writers Transcend Fear.* New York: Henry Holt & Company, 1995.

Lamott, Anne. *Bird by Bird: Some Instructions on Writing and Life.* New York: Anchor Books, 1994.

Langer, Ellen J. *The Psychology of Control.* Beverly Hills: Sage Publications, 1983.

Lao-tzu. *Tao te ching.* Trans Stephen Mitchell. New York: HarperPerennial, 1991.

Leonard, George. *Mastery: The Keys to Success and Long-term Ful-fillment.* New York: Penguin, 1991.

Levine, Peter A. *Waking the Tiger: Healing Trauma.* North Atlantic Books, 1997.

Lowen, Alexander. *Pleasure: A Creative Approach to Life.* New York: Penguin Books, 1970.

Lowen, Alexander. *Depression and the Body: The Biological Basis of Faith and Reality.* New York: Penguin Arkana, 1972.

Lowen, Alexander. *Fear of Life.* New York: Collier Books, 1980.

Lowen, Alexander. *The Spirituality of the Body*. New York: Macmillan Publishing Company, 1990.

May, Rollo. *The Courage to Create*. New York: W.W. Norton & Company, 1975.

Miller, James E. *Word, Self, Reality: The Rhetoric of Imagination*. New York: Dodd Mead and Company, Inc., 1972.

Muller, Wayne. *Legacy of the Heart: The Spiritual Advantages of a Painful Childhood*. New York: Simon & Schuster, 1992.

Nachmanovich, Stephen. *Free Play: Improvisation in Life and Art*. New York: Jeremy P. Tarcher/Putnam, 1990.

Niequist, Shauna. *Cold Tangerines: Celebrating the Extraordinary Nature of Everyday Life*. Grand Rapids, MI: Zondervan, 2007.

Perls, Frederick S. *Gestalt Therapy Verbatim*. Lafayette, CA: Real People Press, 1969.

Perls, Frederick S. *In and Out of the Garbage Pail*. New York: Bantam Books, 1969.

Persig, Robert M. *Zen and the Art of Motorcycle Maintenance*. New York: Bantam Books, 1974.

Putney, Snell & Gail J. Putney. *The Adjusted American: Normal Neuroses in the Individual and Society*. New York: Harper & Row, 1964.

Salzberg, Susan. *Faith: Trusting your own Deepest Experience.* New York: Riverhead Books, 2002.

Trungpa, Chogyam. *Cutting through Spiritual Materialism.* Boston, MA: Shambhala Publication, 1973.

Viorst, Judith. *Imperfect Control: Our Lifelong Struggles with Power and Surrender.* New York: Simon & Schuster, 1998.

Viscott, David. *The Language of Feelings.* New York: Pocket Books, 1977.

Watts, Alan. *The Wisdom of Insecurity: A Message for an Age of Anxiety.* NewYork Vintage Books, 1951.

Watts, Alan. Psychotherapy East and West. New York: Ballantine Books, 1961.

Weingarten, Violet. *Intimations of Mortality.* New York: Alfred A. Knopf, 1978.

Yancey, Philip & Dr. Paul Brand. *The Gift of Pain: Why We Hurt and What We Can Do About It.* Grand Rapids, MI: Zondervan Publishing House, 1997.

ACKNOWLEDGMENTS

Thanks for your feedback, suggestions, encouragement, patience and love: Chris Hauptman, Matt Hauptman, Caitlin Trahan, Colleen Wright, Tony Barrera, Dwight Hurst, Alison Louis, Julie MacCallum, Walter Poleman and Rich Szymanski.

Thanks to Elaina Sawitsky, for creating the Monkeytraps logo.

Thanks to Walt Poleman, for encouraging me to include my drawings.

Thanks to Ali Louis, for spreading the word.

Thanks to my clients, for teaching me about control.

Thanks to my groups, for teaching me about relationships.

Thanks to my family, for making me possible.

Thanks to my grandson Wyatt, for being more fun than a barrel of monkeys.

And thanks, Bert, for letting me finally write this thing.

ABOUT THE AUTHOR

STEVE HAUPTMAN is a Gestalt-trained, Buddhist-flavored therapist who has practiced on Long Island for twenty years. He graduated from Adelphi University's School of Social Work, trained at the Gestalt Center of Long Island, and specializes in a unique control-centered approach that integrates elements of psychodynamic, Gestalt, cognitive-behavioral and family systems theory in the treatment of anxiety, depression, addictions, dual disorders, codependency and relationship problems. A leader of Interactive Therapy groups, he is also a cartoonist and creator of the blogs *Monkeytraps: A blog about control*, *Monkey House* (a forum for discussing control issues), and *Bert's Therapy: Adventures of an Inner Monkey.*

Made in the USA
Lexington, KY
02 August 2017